CHRISTIAN PEER SUPPORT SELF HELP PROGRAM

THE

VICTORY

TIPS PROGRAM

Gain Victory over Anxiety and Depression

Free Daily Telephone Support

Crest that mountain in your life!

Welcome to The Victory Tips Program

Since 2004, we have been helping people rise above anxiety and depression. Over the years, many of the people requesting help have been Christian. Thus, we have published this manual that helps people find wholeness using scripture. We want Christians to plainly see that God wants them well, and that He has provided guidance in the Bible on how to be well. If you are not a Christian, we suggest they find a mature Christian to walk them through this manual. We would be happy to help you find such a person in your area. Our contact information is provided below.

The "Toolbox"

We think of the Bible as a toolbox. But if we don't know how to use the tools in the toolbox, the toolbox will have no value to us. Because many people do not have experience using the "toolbox" (the Bible), we have written the Victory Tips Program in simple terms so it can be easily understood, and be helpful to as many people as possible.

The Program

The Victory Tips Program has three main sections, the 29 Happiness Tips, the Happiness Basics, and the Practical Tools section. The program is written in a recovery group format. This means it can be used to lead a recovery group. People with limited understanding of achieving good mental health can use this program to make a difference in the lives of those around them.

An important benefit of the Victory Tips Program is access to daily support. Daily contact through conference calls and one-to-one support calls enables individuals to quickly learn recovery truths that will help them heal emotionally. The calls also help form friendships. Join calls 7 days a week at 929-205-6099 (US) or 647-558-0588 (Canada), use ID 4578104950, at 7 pm EST.

The Version

The magazine you are reading is a sample of the program that uses Bible verses from the New American Standard Version of the Bible. We also have an edition of the program that uses Bible verses from the King James Version of the Bible. For a copy of the full version, go to www.victorytipsprogram.com.

The Impact

To get the most out of this Bible-based program, we suggest you invite the "Author" of the Bible, Jesus Christ, into your reading time. You can do this by praying this prayer. "Jesus, I invite you into my reading time. Please teach me how to live my life free of all anxiety and depression. Amen."

Please Note

The Victory Tips Program is a peer-to-peer, personal networking and group recovery tool, and is not intended to take the place of professional counseling or medical treatment.

"But thanks be to God, who gives us the victory through our Lord Jesus Christ." 1 Corinthians 15:57

Table of Contents

Faith and Love Publishing 95 Church St., St. Catharines, Ontario, Canada, L2R 3C7

"The only thing that counts is faith expressing itself through love." Galatians 5:6 NIV

ISBN 978-1-7752298-4-1

www.victorytipsprogram.com

"When I first contacted Victory Tips, I was angry, sad, and inconsolable. To say I was difficult is an understatement. I felt cheated and robbed of what had been a happy life. But they more than hung in with me, offering compassion, understanding, and solutions so I could go on…….. Today, I am self-employed which is something I thought I could never do. I can't thank them enough for saving my life and giving me the tools and insight to regain control of my life. They helped me realize there is life after suffering." - Beth (2007)

"My needs as a wife and mother were not being met, and I felt hurt, betrayed, neglected, and at times like I didn't matter. I began shaking and jerking on my left side due to the depression and the medications. I wanted the pain to stop…….. I am now in a church that provides help and support….. For many years I felt like damaged goods. I am being restored. It is by the relationship I have with God that is allowing this to happen. Situations and circumstances are going to come up. I need to remember that I can do all things through Christ who gives me strength." - Lindsay (2006)

"I got back an email that said, "I want to talk to you." I was very hesitant, but unconsciously I must have emailed them back. Then another email came saying that God's will is that you enjoy life. It was as if God himself was speaking to me through those words…….. The things that helped me so much were the Affirmations. I read them every day without fail. Sometimes I read them repeatedly. I apply the Affirmations to my everyday life….. With a whole heart, I gladly endorse the wonderful knowledge and topics that you will find in this program. I trust it will do for you what it did for me. I pray that you give them a chance to help you. Remember that you are not alone. The best is yet ahead of you! The Holy Spirit will embrace you and restore you!"- Lori (2004)

"I found Victory Tips through a telephone prayer line; they were my last hope, I had called every single prayer line listed on the Internet and prayed with thousands of them. My husband of 14 years (17 years of being together) had kicked me out and had replaced me with a girlfriend half his age. We have three children; we had a beautiful farm, everyone thought we were as in love as I thought we were, it crushed me…. This program, the group members, the Lord Christ, God JEHOVAH, saved my life and taught me how to have faith in God and rely on Him to get me through trials, there aren't enough good things I can say about this program." - Sarah (2015)

"I was at an ultimate low in my life when I came to the Victory Tips Program. I had just recently tried to harm myself and was told I needed help. My daughter had found the Victory Tips program online. It was then I decided to try this program. As I began to study this course, I began drawing closer to God after being estranged from him for sooo long. I felt an indescribable PEACE set in. I highly recommend this program to anyone and everyone. This program gives you exactly what the title says, "Victory Tips" on how to cope with life and its challenges !!!! While bringing you closer to God."- Connie (2015)

"My husband and I went through tough times with my family. We also had very stressful financial problems and health problems…. It is a huge blessing of God to have this kind of support that helps me to understand that my real family is my brothers and sisters in Christ… I have received so much love from this program and group that every day I feel so full of the love of God, and that is all that we need to live in Victory. The Victory Tips program itself can heal you, transform you, and change you for the better."- Maribel (2017) "I don't know of anything else that could have helped me through such sorrow as well as this Holy Spirit led program. Victory Tips is amazing. Because of their dedication and diligence, this program lifted me to a higher place in my Christian walk and pulled me out of the loneliness of depression. It also brought much restoration in my family and a closer relationship with Our Lord."- Catherine (2014)

"On reflection, it had been a very brief courtship, and on the day we married my husband's personality immediately appeared to change…He became extremely angry, moody, abusive and at times threatening and violent to me. I knew he had problems, but did not know the extent of them or the possible repercussions…During this desperate time, I became aware of the existence of Victory Tips prayer ministry. We had daily discussions, which probably kept me alive and kept me praying. They linked me with other similar girls on the program with shared prayer calls; this was also supportive to me… I found the Victory tips program literally to be a lifesaver."- Deborah (2015)

"As I explored churches over a period of some 42 years, I was amazed that in the face of the Great Commission, the practical value of making disciples was nearly totally absent. Searching for something to fill that gap in my life I turned to the Victory Tips program. There I found that in the context of the lesson was how to be a disciple of Jesus Christ. The Great Commission must be completed, and discipleship is the first step. "Do your best to present yourself to God as one approved, a worker who does not need to be ashamed and who correctly handles the word of truth (2 Timothy 2:15)." In His love and Service." - David (2019)

"Thirteen years ago I prayed to God to send me someone I could talk to but found no one. I was desperate and did not stop crying. I asked God, "Why?..." all the time. My family thought I had left the best thing that had ever happened to me, and they did not come around. My friends had left because of the man I was with. I searched for help….I found Victory Tips. They understood and listened to me while I cried. They prayed for me, talked to me. They encouraged me to get back to church. I did not want to trust anyone in church again. I listened, and found a church. I changed my thinking…. They were active in my steps to recovery. The Victory Tips Program was the basis of finding the Love of God who heals all of the sorrows in this world. I felt like God would not ever love me as I had been such a sinner. I had to step out in faith and seek His love. Our Lord is faithful to His Word." - Hope (2017)

The numbered paragraphs below are to be read by the participants in the meeting. They will direct the content of the conversation during the meeting.

1 - Chairperson: Welcome everyone to the Victory Tips Recovery Group! My name is ____(Chairperson name)____, and I will be the Chairperson for our meeting. Before we start, please turn off the ringers on your cell phone. Also, please try to limit background noise during the call. Use the Mute feature if need be.

2 - Chairperson: Do we have any new visitors? [If so, kindly acknowledge and thank them for joining in, and ask who wants to participate or just listen in.] Our meetings have two main sections: The Happiness Basics, and the Happiness Tips. As we go through the program, I will read from the bold italics text marked 'Chairperson', and I will call on others who wish to have Speaker Roles by reading from the Bold Arial font text. Please keep your comments to about thirty seconds so everyone has a chance to speak. The last fifteen minutes are reserved for Prayer Requests and members praying for each other. We should finish in 90 min.

3 - Chairperson: So, let's get started! [Chairperson or attendee reads the Recovery Prayer below].

Recovery Prayer

"Dear God, thank you for giving us your Word to heal us. We joyfully dedicate this time to renew our minds to the truths in your Word. With your help we will use your Word to bring down strongholds of fear and deception. We agree that your Word is a light to our path and it leads us to a place of peace, confidence and happiness. We thank you in advance for everything you have done for us, and will do in our lives. You have made our future bright, and we praise you for this. In Jesus's name. Amen."

4 - Chairperson: This program promotes confidentiality. We teach its importance so those unfamiliar with it can learn about it and begin abiding by it. Whatever is said in the group stays in the group. Here to read our Confidentiality Commitment is our first speaker _____(Speaker name)_____.

5 - Confidentiality Speaker: Thank you, ____(Chairperson name)_____.

Confidentiality Commitment

"We value your confidentiality. Whatever we hear you say at a group or in private conversation we promise not to repeat to anyone. This includes your contact information. We will never share any information about you without your permission."

6 - Chairperson: Thank you, _____(Speaker name)_____. We will now hear some praise reports. [Chairperson now asks each person who wants to participate if they have any Praise Reports.]

7 - Chairperson: We will now give a quick overview of how to achieve happiness by using the Happiness Basics. God wants us to be Happy. To talk more about this, is our Happiness Speaker, _(Speaker name)_.

8 – Happiness Speaker: Thank you, ___(Chairperson name)___. Indeed, God wants us to enjoy our journey in life, as seen in the following verses. I will pick one to read, and speak briefly on how it applies to God wanting us to be happy. The verse I choose is _____.

1) **Psalm 19:8** "The precepts of the Lord are right, rejoicing the heart; The commandment of the Lord is pure, enlightening the eyes."

2) **Psalm 28:7** "The Lord is my strength and my shield; My heart trusts in Him, and I am helped; Therefore my heart exults, And with my song I shall thank Him."

3) **Psalm 30:11,12** "You have turned for me my mourning into dancing; You have loosed my sackcloth and girded me with gladness, That my soul may sing praise to You and not be silent. O Lord my God, I will give thanks to You forever."

4) **Psalm 32:11** "Be glad in the Lord and rejoice, you righteous ones; And shout for joy, all you who are upright in heart."

5) **Psalm 64:10** "The righteous man will be glad in the Lord and will take refuge in Him; And all the upright in heart will glory."

6) **Psalm 89:16** "In Your name they rejoice all the day, And by Your righteousness they are exalted."

7) **Psalm 97:11** "Light is sown like seed for the righteous And gladness for the upright in heart."

8) **Ecclesiastes 2:26** "For to a person who is good in His sight He has given wisdom and knowledge and joy,"

9) **Ecclesiastes. 5:19** "Furthermore, as for every man to whom God has given riches and wealth, He has also empowered him to eat from them and to receive his reward and rejoice in his labor; this is the gift of God."

10) **Ecclesiastes. 11:8** "Indeed, if a man should live many years, let him rejoice in them all…"

11) **Luke 10:20** (Jesus speaking) "Nevertheless do not rejoice in this, that the spirits are subject to you, but rejoice that your names are recorded in heaven."

12) **John 10:10** "(Jesus speaking) "The thief comes only to steal and kill and destroy; I came that they may have life, and have it abundantly."

13) **John 15:11** "(Jesus speaking) "These things I have spoken to you so that My joy may be in you, and that your joy may be made full."

14) **Acts 2:25, 26** "For David says of Him, 'I saw the Lord always in my presence; For He is at my right hand, so that I will not be shaken. 'Therefore my heart was glad and my tongue exulted; Moreover my flesh also will live in hope;"

15) **Romans 15:13** "Now may the God of hope fill you with all joy and peace in believing, so that you will abound in hope by the power of the Holy Spirit."

16) **1 Corinthians 15:57** "but thanks be to God, who gives us the victory through our Lord Jesus Christ."

17) **2 Corinthians 2:14** "But thanks be to God, who always leads us in triumph in Christ…"

18) **Galatians 5:22** "But the fruit of the Spirit is love, joy, peace, patience, kindness, goodness, faithfulness",

19) **Philippians 1:25** "Convinced of this, I know that I will remain and continue with you all for your progress and joy in the faith,"

20) **Philippians 4:4** "Rejoice in the Lord always: again I will say, Rejoice."

21) **1 Thessalonians** 5:16 "Rejoice always;"

22) **1 John 1:4** "These things we write, so that our joy may be made complete."

23) **2 John 1:12** "Though I have many things to write to you, I do not want to do so with paper and ink; but I hope to come to you and speak face to face, so that your joy may be made full."

9 - Happiness Speaker: So, God wants us to be happy. We can even be happy when we have problems in our lives. From the verses below, I will pick one to read, and speak briefly on how it applies to us being happy even when we have problems in our lives. The verse I choose is _____.

1) **Psalm 27:6** "And now my head will be lifted up above my enemies around me, And I will offer in His tent sacrifices with shouts of joy; I will sing, yes, I will sing praises to the Lord."

2) **Psalm 119:143** "Trouble and anguish have come upon me, Yet Your commandments are my delight."

3) **Luke 6:22,23** "Blessed are you when men hate you, and ostracize you, and insult you, and scorn your name as evil, for the sake of the Son of Man. 23 Be glad in that day and leap for joy, for behold, your reward is great in heaven. For in the same way their fathers used to treat the prophets."

4) **John 16:33** (Jesus speaking) "These things I have spoken to you, so that in Me you may have peace. In the world you have tribulation, but take courage; I have overcome the world."

5) **Romans 5:3-5a** "And not only this, but we also exult in our tribulations, knowing that tribulation brings about perseverance; and perseverance, proven character; and proven character, hope; and hope does not disappoint,"

6) **Romans 8:18** "For I consider that the sufferings of this present time are not worthy to be compared with the glory that is to be revealed to us."

7) **Romans 8:28** "And we know that God causes all things to work together for good to those who love God, to those who are called according to His purpose."

8) **2 Corinthians 4:17** "For momentary, light affliction is producing for us an eternal weight of glory far beyond all comparison,"

9) **2 Corinthians 7:4** "Great is my confidence in you; great is my boasting on your behalf. I am filled with comfort; I am overflowing with joy in all our affliction."

10) **2 Corinthians 12:9,10** (In this passage, Paul was troubled by a 'thorn in his flesh.') "And He (Jesus) has said to me, "My grace is sufficient for you, for power is perfected in weakness." 10 Most gladly, therefore, I will rather boast about my weaknesses, so that the power of Christ may dwell in me. Therefore I am well content with weaknesses, with insults, with distresses, with persecutions, with difficulties, for Christ's sake; for when I am weak, then I am strong."

11) **Colossians 1:11** "strengthened with all power, according to His glorious might, for the attaining of all steadfastness and patience; joyously."

12) **James 1:2** "Consider it all joy, my brethren, when you encounter various trials,"

13) **1 Peter 1:6** "In this you greatly rejoice, even though now for a little while, if necessary, you have been distressed by various trials,"

14) **1 Peter 3:14** "But and if ye suffer for righteousness' sake, happy are ye: and be not afraid of their terror, neither be troubled;"

15) **1 Peter 4:12,13** "Beloved, do not be surprised at the fiery ordeal among you, which comes upon you for your testing, as though some strange thing were happening to you;. 13 but to the degree that you share the sufferings of Christ, keep on rejoicing, so that also at the revelation of His glory you may rejoice with exultation."

16) **1 Peter 4:14** "If you are reviled for the name of Christ, you are blessed, because the Spirit of glory and of God rests on you."

10 - Happiness Speaker: So even in troubles, we can be happy! Back to you, _(Chairperson_name)_.

11 - Chairperson: Thank you, ____(Speaker name)____. So, it is God's will that we be happy, but it goes deeper than that. God wants us to be strong in our spirit. Here to tell us more on that is our Strong Speaker, ____(Speaker name)____.

12 - Strong Speaker: Thank you, ___(Chairperson name)_____. Indeed, God wants people to be strong in spirit, and from the verses below, I will pick one to read, and speak briefly on how it applies to us being strong in our spirit. The verse I choose is _____.

1) **Joshua 1:6** "Be strong and courageous, for you shall give this people possession of the land which I swore to their fathers to give them."

2) **Joshua 1:7** "Only be strong and very courageous; be careful to do according to all the law which Moses My servant commanded you; do not turn from it to the right or to the left, so that you may have success wherever you go."

3) **Joshua 1:9** "Have I not commanded you? Be strong and courageous! Do not tremble or be dismayed, for the Lord your God is with you wherever you go."

4) **2 Samuel 22:33** "God is my strong fortress; And He sets the blameless in His way."

5) **2 Samuel 22:40** "For You have girded me with strength for battle; You have subdued under me those who rose up against me."

6) **Psalm 31:24** "Be strong and let your heart take courage, All you who hope in the Lord."

7) **Proverbs 24:5** "A wise man is strong, And a man of knowledge increases power."

8) **Romans 8:37** "But in all these things we overwhelmingly conquer through Him who loved us."

9) **1 Corinthians 16:13** "Be on the alert, stand firm in the faith, act like men, be strong."

10) **Ephesians 1:19** "and what is the surpassing greatness of His power toward us who believe. These are in accordance with the working of the strength of His might"

11) **Ephesians 3:16** "that He would grant you, according to the riches of His glory, to be strengthened with power through His Spirit in the inner man,"

12) **Ephesians 3:20** "Now to Him who is able to do far more abundantly beyond all that we ask or think, according to the power that works within us,"

13) **Ephesians 6:10-11** "Finally, be strong in the Lord and in the strength of His might. 11 Put on the full armor of God, so that you will be able to stand firm against the schemes of the devil."

14) **Philippians 4:13** "I can do all things through Him who strengthens me."

15) **Colossians 1:10-11** "so that you will walk in a manner worthy of the Lord, to please Him in all respects, bearing fruit in every good work and increasing in the knowledge of God; strengthened with all power, according to His glorious might, for the attaining of all steadfastness and patience; joyously…"

16) **2 Timothy 1:7** "For God has not given us a spirit of timidity, but of power and love and discipline."

17) **2 Timothy 2:1** "You therefore, my son, be strong in the grace that is in Christ Jesus."

18) **1 Peter 5:10** "After you have suffered for a little while, the God of all grace, who called you to His eternal glory in Christ, will Himself perfect, confirm, strengthen and establish you."

13 - Strong Speaker: So, God wants us to be strong emotionally, but it goes deeper than that. God wants us to stand firm and steadfast, and be bold, established, and confident! From the verses below, I will pick one to read, then share briefly on how it ties in to God wanting us to be stedfast, bold, established and confident. The verse I choose is _____.

1) **Psalm 20:8** "They have bowed down and fallen, But we have risen and stood upright."

2) **Psalm 138:3** "On the day I called, You answered me; You made me bold with strength in my soul."

3) **Proverbs 10:25** "When the whirlwind passes, the wicked is no more, But the righteous has an everlasting foundation."

4) **1 Corinthians 15:58** "Therefore, my beloved brethren, be steadfast, immovable, always abounding in the work of the Lord, knowing that your toil is not in vain in the Lord."

5) **1 Corinthians 16:13** "Be on the alert, stand firm in the faith, act like men, be strong."

6) **2 Corinthians 5:6,8** "Therefore, being always of good courage, and knowing that while we are at home in the body we are absent from the Lord. 8 we are of good courage, I say, and prefer rather to be absent from the body and to be at home with the Lord."

7) **2 Corinthians 7:4** "Great is my confidence in you; great is my boasting on your behalf. I am filled with comfort; I am overflowing with joy in all our affliction."

8) **Ephesians 3:12** "In whom we have boldness and confident access through faith in Him."

9) **Ephesians 3:13** "Therefore I ask you not to lose heart at my tribulations on your behalf, for they are your glory."

10) **Ephesians 3:16** "that He would grant you, according to the riches of His glory, to be strengthened with power through His Spirit in the inner man,"

11) **Ephesians 6:13** "Therefore, take up the full armor of God, so that you will be able to resist in the evil day, and having done everything, to stand firm."

12) **Ephesians. 6:19** "and pray on my behalf, that utterance may be given to me in the opening of my mouth, to make known with boldness the mystery of the gospel,"

13) **Philippians 1:6** "For I am confident of this very thing, that He who began a good work in you will perfect it until the day of Christ Jesus."

14) **Philippians 1:20** "according to my earnest expectation and hope, that I will not be put to shame in anything, but that with all boldness, Christ will even now, as always, be exalted in my body, whether by life or by death."

15) **Philippians 1:27** "Only conduct yourselves in a manner worthy of the gospel of Christ, so that whether I come and see you or remain absent, I will hear of you that you are standing firm in one spirit, with one mind striving together for the faith of the gospel;"

16) **Philippians 4:1** "Therefore, my beloved brethren whom I long to see, my joy and crown, in this way stand firm in the Lord, my beloved."

17) **Colossians 1:23** "if indeed you continue in the faith firmly established and steadfast, and not moved away from the hope of the gospel that you have heard, which was proclaimed in all creation under heaven, and of which I, Paul, was made a minister."

18) **Colossians 2:7** "having been firmly rooted and now being built up in Him and established in your faith, just as you were instructed, and overflowing with gratitude."

19) **1 Thessalonians 3:8** "or now we really live, if you stand firm in the Lord."

20) **1 Thessalonians. 3:13** "so that He may establish your hearts without blame in holiness before our God and Father at the coming of our Lord Jesus with all His saints."

21) **2 Thessalonians 2:15** "So then, brethren, stand firm and hold to the traditions which you were taught, whether by word of mouth or by letter from us."

22) **2 Thessalonians 2:16,17** "Now may our Lord Jesus Christ Himself and God our Father, who has loved us and given us eternal comfort and good hope by grace, comfort and strengthen your hearts in every good work and word."

23) **2 Peter 1:12** "Therefore, I will always be ready to remind you of these things, even though you already know them, and have been established in the truth which is present with you."

24) **James 5:8** "You too be patient; strengthen your hearts, for the coming of the Lord is near."

14 - Strong Speaker: So, God wants us to stand firm and steadfast, and be bold, established and confident. Back to you, ____(Chairperson name)____.

15 - Chairperson: Thank you, ____(Speaker name)____. If God's will is for us to be happy and strong, what do you think gets in the way of us experiencing these attributes in our lives? Hosea 4:6 gives us a clue: It says, "My people are destroyed for a lack of knowledge." Knowledge is powerful. Here to help us understand the importance of gathering knowledge is our Knowledge Speaker, ___(Speaker name)___.

16 - Knowledge Speaker: Thank you, ___(Chairperson name)___. God urges us to gain knowledge, and from the verses below, I will pick one to read, and then speak briefly on how it applies to the importance of gathering knowledge. The verse I choose is _____.

1) King Solomon prayed to God for wisdom and knowledge when he was crowned king.

2 Chronicles 1:9-12 "Now, O Lord God, let thy promise unto David my father be established: for thou hast made me king over a people like the dust of the earth in multitude. 10 Give me now wisdom and knowledge, that I may go out and come in before this people: for who can judge this thy people, that is so great? 11 And God said to Solomon, Because this was in thine heart, and thou hast not asked riches, wealth, or honour, nor the life of thine enemies, neither yet hast asked long life; but hast asked wisdom and knowledge for thyself, that thou mayest judge my people, over whom I have made thee king:12 Wisdom and knowledge is granted unto thee; and I will give thee riches, and wealth, and honour, such as none of the kings have had that have been before thee, neither shall there any after thee have the like."

2) **Proverbs 2:3-5** "For if you cry for discernment, Lift your voice for understanding; If you seek her as silver And search for her as for hidden treasures; Then you will discern the fear of the Lord And discover the knowledge of God "

3) **Proverbs 3:13,14** "How blessed is the man who finds wisdom And the man who gains understanding. For her profit is better than the profit of silver And her gain better than fine gold."

4) **Proverbs 3:20-22** "By His knowledge the deeps were broken up And the skies drip with dew. My son, let them not vanish from your sight; Keep sound wisdom and discretion, So they will be life to your soul And adornment to your neck."

5) **Proverbs 4:1** "Hear, O sons, the instruction of a father, And give attention that you may gain understanding,"

6) **Proverbs 4:5-7** "Acquire wisdom! Acquire understanding! Do not forget nor turn away from the words of my mouth. "Do not forsake her, and she will guard you; Love her, and she will watch over you. "The beginning of wisdom is: Acquire wisdom; And with all your acquiring, get understanding."

7) **Proverbs 4:13** "Take hold of instruction; do not let go. Guard her, for she is your life."

8) **Proverbs 8:5** "O naive ones, understand prudence; And, O fools, understand wisdom."

9) **Proverbs 8:10** "Take my instruction and not silver, And knowledge rather than choicest gold."

10) **Proverbs 16:16** "How much better it is to get wisdom than gold! And to get understanding is to be chosen above silver."

11) **Proverbs 18:15** "The mind of the prudent acquires knowledge, And the ear of the wise seeks knowledge"

12) **Proverbs 23:23** "Buy truth, and do not sell it, Get wisdom and instruction and understanding."

13) **Proverbs 24:3-5** "By wisdom a house is built, And by understanding it is established; 4 And by knowledge the rooms are filled With all precious and pleasant riches. 5 A wise man is strong, And a man of knowledge increases power."

14) **Proverbs 24:14** "Know that wisdom is thus for your soul; If you find it, then there will be a future, And your hope will not be cut off."

17 - Knowledge Speaker: So knowledge is valuable and vital for healing from anxiety and depression. Back to you, ___(Chairperson name)___.

18 - Chairperson: Thank you, ____(Speaker name)____. This program places a great emphasis on God's Word as our way toward peace and happiness. Here to help us understand the importance of God's Word is our Word Speaker, ____(Speaker name)____.

19 - Word Speaker: Thank you, ____(Chairperson name)____. God's Word is very important, and from the verses below, I will pick one to read, and speak briefly on how it applies to the importance God's Word. The verse I choose is _____.

1) Psalm 107:20 He sent His word and healed them, And delivered them from their destructions."

2) The longest psalm in the Bible is Psalm 119. It has 176 verses! It is 2 ½ times longer than the next longest Psalm. The whole psalm talks about God's Word, how the writer loves God's Word. Do you think God is trying to teach us something about the importance of His Word?

3) **Psalm 138:2** I will bow down toward Your holy temple And give thanks to Your name for Your lovingkindness and Your truth; For You have magnified Your word according to all Your name."

4) **Proverbs 4:4** "Then he taught me and said to me, "Let your heart hold fast my words; Keep my commandments and live;"

5) **Isaiah 55:11** "So will My word be which goes forth from My mouth; It will not return to Me empty, Without accomplishing what I desire, And without succeeding in the matter for which I sent it.'"

6) **Luke 6:47-48** "Everyone who comes to Me and hears My words and acts on them, I will show you whom he is like: he is like a man building a house, who dug deep and laid a foundation on the rock; and when a flood occurred, the torrent burst against that house and could not shake it, because it had been well built."

7) **John 1:1** "In the beginning was the Word, and the Word was with God, and the Word was God."

8) **John 8:37** Jesus told us how important God's Word is in John 8:37, saying, "I know that you are Abraham's descendants; yet you seek to kill Me, because My word has no place in you."

9) **John 15:7** Jesus told us how important God's Word is in John 15:7, saying, "If you abide in Me, and My words abide in you, ask whatever you wish, and it will be done for you."

10) **John 17:17** "Sanctify them in the truth; Your word is truth." (God's Word is truth. And we know that the truth sets us free!)

11) **Ephesians 6:17** "And take the helmet of salvation, and the sword of the Spirit, which is the word of God." (You have to know the Word before you can use it!)

20 - Word Speaker: **God's Word is important. But, building God's Word into our hearts, is equally important. From the verses below, I will pick one to read, and speak briefly on how it applies to the importance of building God's Word into our hearts. I choose verse _____.**

1) **Exodus 13:9** "And it shall serve as a sign to you on your hand, and as a reminder on your forehead, that the law of the Lord may be in your mouth; for with a powerful hand the Lord brought you out of Egypt."

2) **Deuteronomy 6:6-9** "These words, which I am commanding you today, shall be on your heart. 7 You shall teach them diligently to your sons and shall talk of them when you sit in your house and when you walk by the way and when you lie down and when you rise up. 8 You shall bind them as a sign on your hand and they shall be as frontals on your forehead. 9 You shall write them on the doorposts of your house and on your gates."

3) **Joshua 1:8** "This book of the law shall not depart from your mouth, but you shall meditate on it day and night, so that you may be careful to do according to all that is written in it; for then you will make your way prosperous, and then you will have success."

4) **Psalm 1:2-3** "But his delight is in the law of the Lord, And in His law he meditates day and night. He will be like a tree firmly planted by streams of water, Which yields its fruit in its season And its leaf does not wither; And in whatever he does, he prospers."

5) **Psalm 119:11** "Your word I have treasured in my heart, That I may not sin against You." (Memorizing scripture can help us live "sin-free".)

6) **Proverbs 2:1** "My son, if you will receive my words And treasure my commandments within you, Make your ear attentive to wisdom, Incline your heart to understanding; For if you cry for discernment, Lift your voice for understanding; If you seek her as silver And search for her as for hidden treasures; Then you will discern the fear of the Lord And discover the knowledge of God."

7) **Proverbs 4:4** "Then he taught me and said to me, "Let your heart hold fast my words Keep my commandments and live;" (Memorize scripture "and live.")

8) **Proverbs 4:20,21** "My son, give attention to my words; Incline your ear to my sayings. Do not let them depart from your sight; Keep them in the midst of your heart."

9) **Jeremiah 20:9** "But if I say, "I will not remember Him Or speak anymore in His name," Then in my heart it becomes like a burning fire Shut up in my bones; And I am weary of holding it in, And I cannot endure it."

10) **Luke 4:1-4** Jesus used God's Word to defend himself when he was tempted by the devil: Jesus, full of the Holy Spirit, returned from the Jordan and was led around by the Spirit in the wilderness for forty days, being tempted by the devil. And He ate nothing during those days, and when they had ended, He became hungry.

And the devil said to Him, "If You are the Son of God, tell this stone to become bread." And Jesus answered him, "It is written, 'Man shall not live on bread alone.'"

11) **Luke 4:5-8** "And he led Him up and showed Him all the kingdoms of the world in a moment of time. And the devil said to Him, "I will give You all this domain and its glory; for it has been handed over to me, and I give it to whomever I wish. Therefore if You worship before me, it shall all be Yours." Jesus answered him, "It is written, 'You shall worship the Lord your God and serve Him only.'"

12) **Luke 4:9-13** "And he led Him to Jerusalem and had Him stand on the pinnacle of the temple, and said to Him, "If You are the Son of God, throw Yourself down from here; for it is written, 'He will command His angels concerning You to guard You,' and, 'On their hands they will bear You up, So that You will not strike Your foot against a stone.'" And Jesus answered and said to him, "It is said, 'You shall not put the Lord your God to the test.'" When the devil had finished every temptation, he left Him until an opportune time."

13) **Luke 6:43-45** "or there is no good tree which produces bad fruit, nor, on the other hand, a bad tree which produces good fruit. For each tree is known by its own fruit. For men do not gather figs from thorns, nor do they pick grapes from a briar bush. The good man out of the good treasure of his heart brings forth what is good; and the evil man out of the evil treasure brings forth what is evil; for his mouth speaks from that which fills his heart."

14) **Luke 6:49** "But the one who has heard and has not acted accordingly, is like a man who built a house on the ground without any foundation; and the torrent burst against it and immediately it collapsed, and the ruin of that house was great."

15) **John 1:14** "And the Word became flesh, and dwelt among us, and we saw His glory, glory as of the only begotten from the Father, full of grace and truth."

16) **John 8:31,32** "So Jesus was saying to those Jews who had believed Him, "If you continue in My word, then you are truly disciples of Mine; and you will know the truth, and the truth will make you free."

17) **Romans 10:8** "But what does it say? "The word is near you, in your mouth and in your heart"—that is, the word of faith which we are preaching,"

18) **Colossians 3:16** "Let the word Christ richly dwell within you, with all wisdom teaching and admonishing one another with psalms and hymns and spiritual songs, singing with thankfulness in your hearts to God."

19) **James 1:21** "Therefore, putting aside all filthiness and all that remains of wickedness, in humility receive the word implanted, which is able to save your souls."

21 - Word Speaker: One cause of emotional pain can be sin. God's Word has an answer for that. From the verses below, I will pick one to read, and speak briefly on how it applies to God having an answer for sin. The verse I choose is number _____.

1) **Psalm 119:2,3** "How blessed are those who observe His testimonies, Who seek Him with all their heart. They also do no unrighteousness They walk in His ways."

2) **Psalm 119:9** "How can a young man keep his way pure? By keeping it according to Your word."

3) **Psalm 119:11** "Your word I have treasured in my heart, That I may not sin against You. (When you memorize God's Word, you are able to recite God's Word throughout your day. By doing so, you are less apt to fall into temptation to sin.)

4) **Psalm 119:127,128** "Therefore I love Your commandments Above gold, yes, above fine gold. Therefore I esteem right all Your precepts concerning everything, I hate every false way."

22 - Word Speaker: Since God's Word is so important, we should ask ourselves: 1) How much time do I spend each day reading and meditating on God's Word? 2) Could it be that my struggles are tied to: a) a lack of interest in God's Word, or b) a lack of understanding of what it teaches about victorious living. Consider praying this prayer: "God, please give me a hunger for your Word." Back to you, ____(Chairperson name)_____.

23 - Chairperson: Thank you, ____(Speaker name)____. Three personal attributes we recommend you develop in your life are: Faith, Truth, and Love. Here to help us understand the importance of Faith, is our Faith Speaker, ___(Speaker name)____.

24 - Faith Speaker: Thank you, ____(Chairperson name)____. The attribute of Faith is an amazing tool. It enables us to roll our problems over to God, thus freeing us up to enjoy life while we wait for God to move on our behalf. The following are Biblical principles that can help us live in Faith, and keep us in a state of constant peace. From the principles below, I will pick one to read, and speak, briefly, on how it helps us live by Faith. I choose Principle number _____.

The Principles Of Faith

1) Based on Hebrews Chapter 11, we see that God places a strong emphasis on a person's faith. **Hebrews 11:6** says, "And without faith it is impossible to please Him, for he who comes to God must believe that He is and that He is a rewarder of those who seek Him."

2) Based on Galatians 5:6, faith works along side of love. **Galatians 5:6** says, "For in Christ Jesus neither circumcision nor uncircumcision means anything, but faith working through love."

3) Based on James 2:26, faith must be demonstrated. (Belief + Action = Faith) **James 2:26** says, "For as the body without the spirit is dead, so faith without works is dead also." **James 2:22** says, "You see that faith was working with his works, and as a result of the works, faith was perfected."

4) Based on Hebrews 10:35,36, faith must be patient. **Hebrews 10:35,36** says, "Therefore, do not throw away your confidence, which has a great reward. For you have need of endurance, so that when you have done the will of God, you may receive what was promised." **Hebrews 6:12** says, "so that you will not be sluggish, but imitators of those who through faith and patience inherit the promises."

5) Based on 2 Corinthians 5:7, we do not judge a problem's solvability by how impossible it looks or how bad we feel. **2 Corinthians 5:7** says, "For we walk by faith, not by sight:"

6) Based on Mark 11:24, we believe we have received the thing we have asked for, even before we actually have it. Jesus says in **Mark 11:24**, "Therefore I say to you, all things for which you pray and ask, believe that you have received them, and they will be granted you." In **Matthew 21:22** He says, "And all things you ask in prayer, believing, you will receive."

7) Based on James 5:15, we see that faith can heal a sick body. **James 5:15** says, "and the prayer offered in faith will restore the one who is sick, and the Lord will raise him up, and if he has committed sins, they will be forgiven him."

8) Based on 1 Timothy 6:12 & Ephesians Chapter 6, we understand that the life of faith is a fight. But based on Romans 8:37, we believe we are more than able to win this fight. **1 Timothy 6:12**

says, "Fight the good fight of faith; take hold of the eternal life to which you were called, and you made the good confession in the presence of many witnesses." **Romans 8:37** says, "But in all these things we overwhelmingly conquer through Him who loved us."

9) Based on James 1:6-8, we see that people who waiver in their faith shouldn't expect to receive anything from God. **James 1:6-8** says, "But he must ask in faith without any doubting, for the one who doubts is like the surf of the sea, driven and tossed by the wind. For that man ought not to expect that he will receive anything from the Lord, being a double-minded man, unstable in all his ways."

10) Based on Romans 10:17, faith must be developed. It does not come naturally. It comes from reading and speaking God's Word. **Romans 10:17** says, "So faith comes from hearing, and hearing by the word of Christ."

25 - Faith Speaker: This principle helps us with _____. Back to you, ___(Chairperson name)___.

26 - Chairperson: Thank you, ____(Chairperson name)____. Here to help us understand the importance of Truth, is our Truth Speaker, ____(Speaker name)____.

27 - Truth Speaker: Thank you, ___(Chairperson name)____. The key verses for the Truth Speaker are John 8:31-32, in which Jesus said to the Jews who had believed in Him: "If you abide in my word, you are truly my disciples, and you will know the truth, and the truth will set you free." Indeed, the Truth can set us free! Circumstances take place in our lives that cause us to believe lies. These lies tell us that problems will never change, habits cannot be broken, loved ones will never change, and so on. The antidote to these lies is Truth. For every problem in our lives there is a Truth that can set us free, emotionally, from the problem. The problem may still be there, but the anxiety related to it is gone. Below are some common lies we sometimes believe. From the lies below, I will pick one to read, and speak, briefly, on how it hinders our happiness, and how the truth can set us free. I will choose lie number ____.

1) God doesn't love me.
2) I could never get married.
3) I could never forgive that person.
4) I could never be healed physically.
5) I could never be happy with my spouse.
6) Nobody would want to be my friend.
7) I need to have a spouse to be happy.
8) I could never be happy in my job.
9) I need money or things to be happy.
10) I'll never progress past this level of success.
11) I need to be loved and accepted to be happy.
12) I could never break free from my addiction.
13) I'll never have what it takes to be gainfully employed.
14) My worrying about problems shows that I am responsible.
15) My past is so bad, I'll never recover from my emotional wounds.
16) I could never be happy without this person. (e.g. A loved one who passes away)
17) I need to change my bodily features to be happy and accepted. (e.g. weight changes or cosmetic surgery.)
18) I need to act a certain way to be happy and accepted. (e.g. "I need to be the life of the party.)

28 - Truth Speaker: By seeing these lies for what they are, and using the Truth of God's Word to renew our minds, we can be set free from these lies! Back to you, ___(Chairperson name)___.

29 - Chairperson: Thank you, ____(Speaker name)____. Here to help us understand the importance of Love, is our Love Speaker, ____(Speaker name)____.

30 - Love Speaker: Thank you, ___(Chairperson name)___. Love helps us respond properly to life's challenges. We may know what we should do, but it is Love that allows us to do it willfully and cheerfully. Love is not based on feelings, but on our commitments. Love is a decision we make each day and is proven by our actions. From the verses below, I will pick one to read, and speak, briefly, on how it applies to the importance of Love. I will choose verse ____.

1) **Romans 13:8** "Owe nothing to anyone except to love one another; for he who loves his neighbor has fulfilled the law."
2) **Matthew 5:43-45** "You have heard that it was said, 'You shall love your neighbor and hate your enemy.' ⁴⁴But I say to you, love your enemies and pray for those who persecute you, ⁴⁵ so that you may be sons of your Father who is in heaven; for He causes His sun to rise on the evil and the good, and sends rain on the righteous and the unrighteous."
3) **1 Corinthians 13:3** "And if I give all my possessions to feed the poor, and if I surrender my body to be burned, but do not have love, it profits me nothing."
4) **1 Corinthians 13:4** "Love is patient, love is kind and is not jealous; love does not brag and is not arrogant,"
5) **1 Corinthians 13:5** "does not act unbecomingly; it does not seek its own, is not provoked, does not take into account a wrong suffered,"
6) **1 Corinthians 13:6** "Love does not rejoice in unrighteousness, but rejoices with the truth;"
7) **1 Corinthians 13:7** "Love bears all things, believes all things, hopes all things, endures all things."
8) **1 Corinthians 13:8** "Love never fails; but if there are gifts of prophecy, they will be done away; if there are tongues, they will cease; if there is knowledge, it will be done away."
9) **1 Corinthians 13:13** "But now faith, hope, love, abide these three; but the greatest of these is love."
10) **Galatians 5:13** "For you were called to freedom, brethren; only do not turn your freedom into an opportunity for the flesh, but through love serve one another."
11) **Galatians 5:14** "For the whole Law is fulfilled in one word, in the statement, "You shall love your neighbor as yourself.""
12) **Galatians 5:22,23** "But the fruit of the Spirit is love, joy, peace, patience, kindness, goodness, faithfulness, gentleness, self-control; against such things there is no law."
13) **Ephesians 4:2** "with all humility and gentleness, with patience, showing tolerance for one another in love,"
14) **1 Peter 1:22** "Since you have in obedience to the truth purified your souls for a sincere love of the brethren, fervently love one another from the heart:"
15) **1 Peter 4:8** "Above all, keep fervent in your love for one another, because love covers a multitude of sins."
16) **1 John 4:7** "Beloved, let us love one another, for love is from God; and everyone who loves is born of God and knows God."
17) **1 John 4:18** "There is no fear in love; but perfect love casts out fear, because fear involves punishment, and the one who fears is not perfected in love."

31 - Love Speaker: So Love is vital to living a happy fruitful life! Back to you, ___(Chairperson name)___.

32 - Chairperson: Thank you, ____(Speaker name)____. Affirmations are designed to be spoken out loud, enabling us to use our own self-help resource, our tongue. Here to help us understand the importance of affirmations is our Affirmations Speaker, ____(Speaker name)____.

33 - Affirmations Speaker: Thank you, ____(Chairperson name)____. As we hear truth spoken by our own mouth, our belief system begins to change. Positive beliefs spawn positive thoughts, and positive thoughts create and maintain happiness. This program offers both generic and Bible-based affirmations. You can even create your own affirmations, customized for situations you come up against. I will pick a Generic Affirmation to read, and share, briefly, how it helps us. The affirmation I choose is ____.

Generic Affirmations

1) "I am bigger than fear."
2) "I bounce back easily."
3) "I live my life effortlessly."
4) "My job is easy."
5) "I handle change easily."
6) "I love a challenge."
7) "Self-discipline is my strong point."
8) "I always see a silver lining."
9) "I see myself as a peaceful, loving person."
10) "You can't upset me. (I won't let you.)"
11) "I see myself as a winner before I see my victory."
12) "I forgive everybody immediately after they hurt me."
13) "God can bring good out of any of my mistakes."
14) "I see my prayers getting answered before I see the actual answer to my prayers."
15) "I see myself as healed in my body before I see and feel the changes I desire."

34 - Affirmations Speaker: I will now choose one of the Bible-based Affirmations below, in which we will all read 3 statements from. The Affirmation I choose is number _____.

Bible-Based Affirmations

1) "I Do Not Fear" Affirmation (Page 19)
2) "I Am Strong" Affirmation (Page 19)
3) "I Flow in Harmony and Love" Affirmation (Page 20)
4) "I Only Speak Right Words" Affirmation (Page 20)
5) "I Only Think Right Thoughts" Affirmation (Page 21)
6) "I Am Happy Because…" Affirmation (Page 21)

35 - Affirmation Speaker: Positive affirmations spoken boldly, define what we believe is true. Doing so positions us to receive more from God and from life! So speak boldly! Back to you, ____(Chairperson name)____.

36 - Chairperson: Thank you, ____(Speaker name)____. Slogans are thought-provoking statements that challenge us to respond to life's problems positively. To tell us more on Slogans is our Slogans Speaker, ____(Speaker name)____.

37 - Slogans Speaker: Thank you, ___(Chairperson name)___. From the slogans below, I will pick one to read, and share, briefly, on how it helps us. The slogan I choose is number____.

1) "Sleep on it."
2) "Don't enable."
3) "I play to win!"
4) "You can start again."
5) "Knowledge is power."
6) "My job is to believe."
7) "Every day's a good day."
8) "Say it until you believe it."
9) "Respond rather than react."
10) "God is bigger than the facts!"
11) "We live by faith, not by sight."
12) "When we're in a battle, we fight!"
13) "Stop running, and start confronting."
14) "It's not my problem, it's God's problem.
15) "Positive believing produces positive thinking."
16) "Faith is a lifestyle I can learn."
17) "Anger can be a sign that you are judging."
18) "God responds to faith, seldom to need."
19) "Don't make their problem, your problem.
20) "Problems are opportunities to see God move."
21) "The best Defense is a strong Offense."
22) "There is a stress-cancelling response to every problem."
23) "Don't focus on what you lost, focus on what you gained!"
24) "Life is 10% what happens to you, 90% how you respond to it."
25) "Problems are inevitable, the stress is optional."

38 - Slogans Speaker: Slogans are quick reminders of the truth. Say them often! Back to you, ____ (Chairperson name)_____.

39 - Chairperson: Thank you, ____(Speaker name)____. There's an easy way to keep our thinking in check. Here to tell us more on that is our Beliefs Speaker, ____(Speaker name)____.

40 - Beliefs Speaker: Thank you, ____(Chairperson name)____. Our thinking is influenced by our beliefs. Positive beliefs help us keep our responses to life's problems positive. We recommend adopting the following six Core Beliefs. The idea is to make these Core Beliefs the final word in our lives. No matter what our feelings say or what the circumstances try to tell us, these foundational beliefs are what we are going to use when thinking about ourselves, and when making decisions in our lives. For any belief that feels untrue, we simply say the scriptures associated with that belief over and over until the belief feels true. I will choose one Core Belief to read 3 verses from. The core belief I pick is number ____.

Core Beliefs

1) "I Believe God loves me, and that I am valuable." (Pg 22)
2) "I Believe Christ's crucifixion paid for my sin." (Pg 22)
3) "I Believe God wants me to live in perfect peace." (Pg 22)
4) "I Believe I have an enemy – Satan." (Pg 23)
5) "I Believe I have another enemy – my fleshly appetites." (Pg 23)
6) "I Believe God wants me to enjoy good physical health." (Pg 23)

41 - Beliefs Speaker: So, adopting and developing this Core Belief will help us with _____. Back to you, ____(Chairperson name)____.

42 - Chairperson: Thank you, ____(Speaker name)____. Our unhappiness can sometimes be easily diagnosed by pinpointing what the hindrance is. Here to talk to us about hindrances to happiness is our Hindrance Speaker, ____(Speaker name)____.

43 - <u>Hindrance Speaker</u>: Thank you, ____(Chairperson name)____. There are many hindrances to happiness. From the hindrances below, I will pick one to read, and speak, briefly, how it affects our happiness. The Hindrance I choose is number ____.

Hindrances

1) Self-pity "If only…"
2) Having an unthankful heart
3) Ostracized by community
4) Double-mindedness
5) Lack of purpose
6) Believing lies
7) Guilt (real or imagined)
8) Entitlement mentality
9) Sin, or sinful thinking
10) Unforgiveness
11) Debt
12) Shame
13) Anger
14) Isolation
15) Perfectionism
16) Lack of patience
17) Physical tiredness
18) Doubt and Unbelief
19) A Rebellious Heart
20) Mourning a loss
21) Pouting "I want it my way!"
22) Having an unthankful heart
23) Leaning on your own intellect
24) Being judgmental toward people.
25) Enabling abusive or poor behavior

44 - <u>Hindrance Speaker</u>: Let's live free of hindrances so we can brightly shine God's love in everything we do! Back to you, ____(Chairperson name)____.

45 - Chairperson: Thank you, ____(Speaker name)____. We'll now work with one of the Happiness Tips. The place we left off last time was Page #____. [If the place isn't known, the Chairperson may choose any Tip, and when finished, bring the group back here.]

(After working a Tip.)

46 - <u>Gospel Speaker</u>: We believe it is important to have a relationship with God, and that this relationship can help us find healing in our emotions. Let's take turns reading the following statements in the order we've been using.
[Chairperson prompts speakers in the existing order.]

1) The main purpose of the Bible is to show mankind their need of Jesus Christ.
2) God wants to fellowship with mankind, but He can't until the issue of their sin has been dealt with.
3) Throughout the Bible there are prophecies about Jesus, and there are stories about Jesus.
4) All of these are there to show us the importance of Jesus.
5) Because of our tendency to sin, we need someone who would pay the penalty of our sin. And that was Jesus.
6) **John 3:16** says, "For God so loved the world, that He gave His]only begotten Son, that whoever believes in Him shall not perish, but have eternal life."
7) **Romans 1:16** says, "For I am not ashamed of the gospel, for it is the power of God for salvation to everyone who believes, to the Jew first and also to the Greek."
8) **Romans 6:23** says, "For the wages of sin is death, but the free gift of God is eternal life in Christ Jesus our Lord."
9) **Romans 5:8** says, "But God demonstrates His own love toward us, in that while we were yet sinners, Christ died for us."
10) Jesus, God's Son, came to earth to show us how to live, and to pay the penalty for our sin by dying on the cross.
11) Once we personally receive forgiveness for our sin, and ask Jesus to guide our lives, we find New Life! And we become part of God's family.
12) **John 3:3** says, "Truly, truly, I say to you, unless one is born again he cannot see the kingdom of God."
13) So, we must be born again. Is there anyone here who would like to become born again? And find New Life! And find forgiveness for their sins and become a part of God's family?

47 - Chairperson: Please read along as I say the invitational prayer below.

"Dear God, I see the sins that I have committed. I believe Jesus paid the penalty for my sin by His crucifixion. I receive your forgiveness for my sin. And I ask you to come into my life, and help me to live the rest of my life in a way that pleases you. Amen."

48 - Congratulations! If you've prayed this prayer sincerely, you are now born again! You are now a part of God's family! And we, as a group, will help you learn how to live a happy, fruitful life in Christ. Welcome to God's family!

49 - Chairperson: For those of us who are already born again, God asks us to tell the world that they can be born again. Here are some verses that bear this out. Let's take turns reading these verses out loud.

13) **Mark 16:15** (Jesus tells us) "Go into all the world and preach the gospel to all creation."
14) **2 Corinthians 5:20** "Therefore, we are ambassadors for Christ, as though God were making an appeal through us; we beg you on behalf of Christ, be reconciled to God."
15) **2 Corinthians 5:18** "Now all these things are from God, who reconciled us to Himself through Christ and gave us the ministry of reconciliation,"
16) **2 Corinthians 5:14** "For the love of Christ controls us, having concluded this, that one died for all, therefore all died;"
17) **2 Corinthians 3:6** "who also made us adequate as servants of a new covenant, not of the letter but of the Spirit; for the letter kills, but the Spirit gives life."

50 - So let's challenge ourselves to tell the Good News of Jesus wherever we go this week. May God help us!

51 - We would like to take time now to pray for each other's needs. [Chairperson asks each person individually if they have any prayer requests, writing each one down, then asks who would like to pray for each person. Then the Chairperson goes back through the list asking each person who offered to pray to do so.]

52 - Does anyone have any final words before we conclude our meeting?

53 - I will now offer a closing prayer...

54 - Our meetings are held *[tell days/times].*

Tip #1 "Fly By the Instruments"

1A - Flying by the Instruments is a term used when aircraft pilots are unable to see ahead of them because of precipitation, darkness, or cloud cover. In these conditions, pilots rely on their instruments to guide them safely to their destination. We thank God for instruments in an aircraft because they can mean the difference between landing safely, and crash landing. So it is in our lives. Life can become so difficult that we can no longer "see where we are going". We end up losing inner peace and happiness. At these times it is vital that we know how to "Fly by the Instruments."

Question 1: Can you remember a time when you needed help to get through a problem? If so, would you like to share with us briefly what happened?

2A - What are the "instruments" we can "fly" by? The scriptures give us principles we can hold onto when life gets tough.

"Instrument No. 1" - God Loves Us.

During most times in our lives, the fact that God loves us may be an unquestionable truth. Here are some scriptures about God's love for us.

a) **John 3:16** "For God so loved the world, that He gave His only begotten Son, that whoever believes in Him shall not perish, but have eternal life."

b) **Ephesians 2:4** "But God, being rich in mercy, because of His great love with which He loved us,"

c) **Titus 3:4** "But when the kindness of God our Savior and His love for mankind appeared,"

2B - However, when we are under severe stress, the simple truth of God's love can seem foreign to us. It can tempt us to believe that God is mad at us,…. *(1,713 more words in full version.)*

Tip #3 - Admit You Have a Problem

1A - This can be a difficult step because it requires us to admit we have a weakness in our life. However, weaknesses can be blessings in disguise. When we conquer a weakness, we increase our self-esteem and we gain the ability to help others who struggle with a similar weakness.

1B - One of the more challenging aspects of this Tip can be facing the extent of our damaged emotions. Most of us do our best to present a positive image to the people we interact with each day. But if we've only learned a few "tricks" to barely get through everyday life, it won't take many life problems to overload our capacity to manage them well. Eventually, the challenges can overpower our cobbled defenses, and we see the true extent of our damaged emotions. This is the risk we take by not dealing with our issues. Now is the time to decide what we want to do. Do we remain a "just-getting-by" person, or do we work at becoming a healed person, someone who genuinely embraces and enjoys all aspects of our life?

Question 1: Do you know people who are "just-getting-by" or "healed and at peace"?

2A - Forced To Learn

Sometimes we don't have the luxury of being able to choose which of the above groups we want to be in; life has already conquered us, and we are forced to learn new ways to win at life. Thankfully, there are benefits to being "down and out".

For one, we have no image to live up to. People have already seen us at our worst, so there's no having to try hard to hide our mental health challenge.

2B – Two, we become a tangible example of recovery to those who know us. Our friends…. *(1,480 more words in full version.)*

Tip #2 - Stop, and Be Still

1A - We can all agree that life can be challenging. When we get to a point where we've been trying so hard to make life work but things aren't going well, sometimes it is good to just stop.

But what does the average person do? They keep trying and trying until they exhaust themselves physically and emotionally. Life was never meant to be so difficult, but we make it so because of our ignorance.

1B - What Does "Stop" Mean?

When life gets hard, and we stop, we're not quitting, we're just pausing to assess our strategies. What does 'Stop' mean to you in your situation? It may mean to stop actions leading to a divorce or a job resignation. Maybe it means cutting back on commitments or working fewer hours. Whatever it may be, we're going to have to stop and take time to learn strategies that can help us win in life.

1C - "Stopping" in the Scriptures

One incident in the scriptures of a person feeling the need to stop was Mary, the sister of Martha. In Luke Chapter 10 we read how Jesus went to Mary and Martha's house to visit and teach them. Mary chose to stop and sit at Jesus's feet to hear Him teach. When Martha complained to Jesus that her sister wasn't helping her prepare food for His visit, Jesus told Martha, that Mary had chosen the right thing to do, to stop and hear him teach. Mary chose to "stop and be still," and it gave her favor with Jesus.

Question 1: What is your favorite place in your home where you can stop and be still each day to learn from the scriptures?

2A - Saul of Tarsus

Another time in…. *(1,473 more words in full version.)*

Tip #4 - Disarm the Shame

1A - As stated in Tip #3, emotional problems can sometimes carry a stigma. So for us to proceed smoothly in our recovery, we may need to disarm shame so it doesn't prevent us from reaching out for help.

We may be hearing a voice in our mind shouting, "Don't tell the family secrets!" But we shouldn't listen to that voice. That voice wants to keep us in bondage. Now is the time to tell what has happened to us. When we tell it to the right people, they will show us how to be set free from anxiety and depression.

Let's look at some Bible verses that show us that God wants us to live free of shame.

a) **Psalm 25:3** "Indeed, none of those who wait for You will be ashamed; Those who deal treacherously without cause will be ashamed."

b) **Psalm 31:1** "In You, O Lord, I have taken refuge; Let me never be ashamed;In Your righteousness deliver me."

c) **Psalm 34:5** "They looked to Him and were radiant, And their faces will never be ashamed."

d) **Psalm 119:80** "May my heart be [a]blameless in Your statutes, So that I will not be ashamed."

e) **Isaiah 54:4** "Fear not, for you will not be put to shame; And do not feel humiliated, for you will not be disgraced; But you will forget the shame of your youth, And the reproach of your widowhood you will remember no more."

f) **Isaiah 61:7** "Instead of your shame you will have a double portion, And instead of humiliation they will shout for joy over their portion. Therefore they will…. *(2,304 more words in full version.)*

Tip #5 - Form a Support Team

1A - In Tip #4 we learned about our need to ask for help. In Tip #5 we will learn what to look for in people who may be able to help us. We'll also learn that it is helpful to choose more than one or two people to help us at this critical time in our lives. The following Bible verses urge us to have many advisers.

a) **Proverbs 11:14** "Where there is no guidance the people fall, But in abundance of counselors there is victory."

b) **Proverbs 15:22** "Without consultation, plans are frustrated, But with many counselors they succeed."

c) **Proverbs 24:6** "For by wise guidance you will [a]wage war, And in abundance of counselors there is victory."

Here is a verse about having helpers in our life.

Ecclesiastes 4:12 "And if one can overpower him who is alone, two can resist him. A cord of three strands is not quickly torn apart."

Question 1: What do you think of the idea of having a network of people in our lives to help us find peace and happiness?

2A - <u>What To Look For</u>

Not everyone can be a support-person in our lives. That is because most people cannot relate to feelings of severe anxiety and depression. Approaching certain people with our request for help can sometimes bring uneasiness to our relationship with them. Therefore, it is best to do a little research on the people we wish to enlist for our support team. Here are a few questions to ask ourselves about a candidate:

a) Do I respect them?

b) Do they have a calm demeanor? *(1,162 more words in full version.)*

Tip #7 - Speak Right Words

1A - Many people do not know that there is a link between the words we speak and the events that take place in our lives. The Bible has many scriptures that teach this truth. One of the better-known scriptures is in the account of the creation of the world. In Genesis 1:3, we read, "Let there be light," and there was light." After this God began to speak into existence, the earth, the water, the animals, and more. He did this by speaking words. We learn from this, that spoken words can have great power.

1B - <u>Jesus and Words</u>

Another well-known scripture on the power in words is Mark 11:23, when Jesus said: "Truly I say to you, whoever says to this mountain, 'Be taken up and cast into the sea,' and does not doubt in his heart, but believes that what he says is going to happen, it will be granted him."

1C - <u>The Book of James and Words</u>

The Book of James also reveals the power of the tongue. James 3:4-5 says, "Look at the ships also, though they are so great and are driven by strong winds, are still directed by a very small rudder wherever the inclination of the pilot desires. So also the tongue is a small part of the body, and yet it boasts of great things."

1D - Then verse 6 paints a very dramatic picture of the power of the tongue when it is allowed to speak negative words in a person's life. James 3:6 says, "And the tongue is a fire, the very world of iniquity; the tongue is set among our members as that which defiles the entire body, and sets on fire the course of our life, and is set on fire by hell."

1E - <u>More Evidence on the Power of Words</u>

There is more power in words than we may think. For instance Proverbs 18:21 says, "Death and…. *(3,301 more words in full version.)*

Tip #6 - Guard Your Thoughts

1A - Thoughts are powerful. Those of us who have trouble with our thinking can relate to the fact that when we let our thoughts go negative, we feel negative. That is going to change. God gives us tips on how to be an overcomer in life. This includes having the ability to think right thoughts!

Below is a profound scripture about our thinking:

Proverbs 23:7 "For as he thinks within himself, so he is."

1B - This verse means our thinking reveals who we are.

Many of us think we are better than who we really are, and that hurts us. As long as we don't see the work that needs to be done in our hearts, we will never be motivated to change what we think and believe. From now on, may God help us see, clearly, who we are. And may we say from now on, "I'm going to work with God to transform my life into the likeness of his Son, the Lord Jesus Christ. Jesus will be manifested in everything I think, say, and do."

1C - The above Bible verse, Proverbs 23:7, tells us we are what we think about. Thus, we must be careful what we believe about ourselves, as this will affect what we think about ourselves.

In the above verse, the term, "heart", refers to our thinking. So we must "Keep" (or guard) our thoughts.

Question 1: Have you ever heard the term "Guard your thoughts?" What comes to mind about this?

2A - <u>What Influences Our Thinking?</u>

Our thinking, be it positive or negative, is the result of experiences we've had in our life. Some of these experiences were caused by our own choices, but many….*(1,311 more words in full version.)*

Tip #8 - Make Right Choices

1A - A railway switch is small, but is capable of sending a huge, heavy train in a completely different direction. Similarly, one small decision can send our life in a completely different direction; many times to heartache and loss. One way to prevent this, is found in the scripture below;

Proverbs 3:5,6 "Trust in the Lord with all your heart And do not lean on your own understanding. In all your ways acknowledge Him, And He will make your paths straight."

It seems simple; ask God to come into our situation and guide us.

Question 1: Are you in the habit of asking God to guide you in all your endeavors?

2A - <u>Seek Assistance</u>

Heartaches begin when life gives us a problem in which we have little knowledge of how to solve it.

Whenever we come to a situation that requires more understanding than what we have, we need to get help. God doesn't want us to "think up" a way out of a problem with just our own limited understanding. More often than not, we will get ourselves into trouble by doing so.

2B - <u>Follow Children</u>

For the most part, children have no worries. All they have to do is, get good grades at school, do a little work around the house, and get along with other kids. They seldom worry about the future, and they rarely get upset over the past. Their focus is more or less on the present. Thus, their stress level is usually low, and their mood is generally good.

Question 2: Have you ever wished you were as happy and carefree as children?

3A - As far as basic needs…. ***(1,156 more words in full version.)***

Tip #9 - Develop Your Faith

1A - At first glance faith seems like a vague, mystical concept, something that we could never truly understand or benefit from. However, the Bible says the opposite. The Bible even calls it a substance. In the 11th Chapter of the Book of Hebrews (the Faith Chapter), the Bible tells us what faith is. Hebrews 11:1 says: "Now faith is the assurance of things hoped for, the conviction of things not seen." In God's realm, faith is important. In fact, faith is the "currency of heaven." It is vital when looking to God for His help in our lives.

1B - So, the Bible calls faith a substance. It may not be something we can touch, but it is something we can see and hear. We see it in people's actions. And we can hear it in people's words.

You Already Use Faith

A simple example of using faith can be in the use of a chair. We see that it looks strong enough to hold our weight, and by the act of sitting on the chair, we show we have faith in it.

1C - Faith is a Choice

We can have strong faith, or we can have weak faith, the choice is ours. Romans 10:17 says "So faith comes from hearing, and hearing by the word of Christ." Faith comes by hearing God's Word. Thus, the more we saturate ourselves in the Bible, the stronger our faith becomes. Developing our faith takes time reading and speaking God's Word. But it starts with a choice, a burning desire to have strong faith.

Question 1: Have you ever met someone who had an unshakable faith in God? If so, have you ever wished you had that same kind of faith?

2A - Faith Got Jesus's Attention

Faith is a noun. But it is…. *(1,564 more words in full version.)*

Tip #10 - Respond Rather Than React

1A - If we were to describe the journey to emotional healing in a single sentence, it would be this: It is the process of learning how to respond to life's challenges, rather than react to them. We need to learn how to slow down our decision-making process when we get caught off guard. This Tip will help us do that.

1B - Natural reactions are great if they are coming from a healthy foundation, but if they are coming from a weak foundation, they can be crippling. If we give somebody struggling with anxiety and depression another situation to juggle in their lives, their natural reaction may be less than helpful. On the other hand, let's compare such a situation to an athlete who trains 4-6 hours daily so they can be their best on game day. Their natural reactions during the game will be practically perfect, and will help them achieve success in their sport.

1C - Start Training!

Just like an athlete who trains each day to improve their athletic abilities, we can also train in the area of our thinking to achieve a greater measure of personal well-being. This kind of training sharpens our ability to respond effectively to stressful situations, and will help us to stay peaceful so we can enjoy every aspect of our day.

Question 1: Do you know someone who trains diligently for any reason?

2A - Who's Causing the Problem?

Have you ever felt totally drained at the end of work days, for days on end? Life can be hard. And it can tempt us to believe that it is our situation or person in our life which is causing our unrest. However, the root problem is usually our improper response to the challenges in our life. That is great news…. *(3,950 more words in full version.)*

Tip #11 - Know Yourself

1A - Life has a way of leading us away from God's best for our lives. The problem is that change in our heart can happen so slowly that we aren't aware we are drifting away from God. What complicates this problem further is that we have inherent weaknesses that we may not be aware of, or not paying attention to. Not being aware of our weaknesses can be a serious problem. Our enemy, the devil, knows us better than we know ourselves, and he can use this knowledge against us. Let's take some time to identify our strengths and weaknesses, so we'll be ready for any challenge that comes our way.

1B - People in the Bible had weaknesses. God has given us their stories so we can learn from them.

Eve was too naïve when she was speaking with the serpent (Satan).

Genesis 3:1-6 "Now the serpent was more crafty than any beast of the field which the Lord God had made. And he said to the woman, "Indeed, has God said, 'You shall not eat from any tree of the garden'?" [2] The woman said to the serpent, "From the fruit of the trees of the garden we may eat; [3] but from the fruit of the tree which is in the middle of the garden, God has said, 'You shall not eat from it or touch it, or you will die.'" [4] The serpent said to the woman, "You surely will not die! [5] For God knows that in the day you eat from it your eyes will be opened, and you will be like God, knowing good and evil." [6] When the woman saw that the tree was good for food, and that it was a delight to the eyes, and that the tree was desirable to make *one* wise, she took from its fruit and ate; and she gave also to her husband with her, and he ate."

1C - Adam's weakness was his impulsiveness to take the fruit from Eve.

Question 1: Does anyone come to mind that is naïve like Eve, or impulsive like Adam? *(1,521 more words in full version.)*

Tip #12 - Don't Judge

1A - One major cause of anxiety and depression is the act of passing judgment on others. You might ask, "Do I just turn a blind eye to anyone that does wrong to me?" That depends on the situation. Every circumstance is different, and every person we come in contact with is different, thus requiring a particular response. Having a pastor or a support team in our life will give us people we can speak with, who can give us suggestions on how to best respond to a given situation.

1B - If it is an abusive situation we should first try to remove ourselves from the abuse. By doing so, we can better assess the hurtful action. We will then be better able to respond properly to it if it happens again. (To recognize abuse more readily, see the "Types of Abuse" section at the end of the book.)

1C - When someone abuses us it is natural to pass judgment on them. However, Jesus tells us not to judge others. Here are two such verses.

a) **Matthew 7:1,2** (Jesus is speaking) "Do not judge so that you will not be judged. 2 For in the way you judge, you will be judged; and by your standard of measure, it will be measured to you."

b) **Luke 6:37** "Do not judge, and you will not be judged; and do not condemn, and you will not be condemned; pardon, and you will be pardoned."

1D - When Jesus tells us not to judge, does that mean we can't judge the action? We know that judicial judges judge actions all the time. We also know that Jesus gives permission to judge people's actions when He says, "Do not give what is holy to dogs, and do not throw your pearls before swine," (**Matthew 7:6**) and "Beware of false prophets" (Matthew 7:15-16). How do we determine who the dogs and pigs are, and the false prophets are if we not allowed to judge?

1E - When we share…. *(1,056 more words in full version.)*

Tip #13 - Be "Good Ground"

1A - Jesus tells us that the parable of the sower is a "stand-alone" parable. He asks, how will you know any parable if you don't know this one? Thus, it is good for us to read it, and glean everything we can from it. The title of this Tip comes from the soil types described in the parable. May God teach us something valuable as we read it.

1B - **Mark 4:3-20**

"Listen *to this*! Behold, the sower went out to sow; [4] as he was sowing, some *seed* fell beside the road, and the birds came and ate it up. [5] Other *seed* fell on the rocky *ground* where it did not have much soil; and immediately it sprang up because it had no depth of soil. [6] And after the sun had risen, it was scorched; and because it had no root, it withered away. [7] Other *seed* fell among the thorns, and the thorns came up and choked it, and it yielded no crop. [8] Other *seeds* fell into the good soil, and as they grew up and increased, they yielded a crop and produced thirty, sixty, and a hundredfold." [9] And He was saying, "He who has ears to hear, let him hear." [10] As soon as He was alone, His followers, along with the twelve, *began* asking Him *about* the parables."

1C - "[11] And He was saying to them, "To you has been given the mystery of the kingdom of God, but those who are outside get everything in parables, [12] so that WHILE SEEING, THEY MAY SEE AND NOT PERCEIVE, AND WHILE HEARING, THEY MAY HEAR AND NOT UNDERSTAND, OTHERWISE THEY MIGHT RETURN AND BE FORGIVEN." [13] And He *said to them, "Do you not understand this parable? How will you understand all the parables? [14] The sower sows the word. [15] These are the ones who are beside the road where the word is sown; and when they hear, immediately Satan comes and takes away the word which has been sown in them."

1D - "[16] In a similar way…. *(229 more words in full version.)*

Tip #15 - Eliminate Wasted Thinking

1A - As we journey toward peace and happiness, we'll need to look at all the ways wasted thinking takes up room in our daily thoughts. In this Tip, we'll explore the various negative ways our mind can think. Then we'll look at ways to disarm these negative thought patterns when they come up.

1B - Types of Wasted Thinking

The following webpage describes 15 ways in which our thinking can be hindered. Please refer to psychcentral.com/lib/15-common-cognitive-distortions and read the introduction.

1C - Filtering

Please read the "Filtering" description at psychcentral.com/lib/15-common-cognitive-distortions.

1D - "Filtering" in the Bible

In 1Samuel 18, we see that even though the shepherd boy, David, killed a giant enemy of Israel, King Saul became angry because the boy became more famous than he.

1 Samuel 18:6-11 "It happened as they were coming, when David returned from killing the Philistine, that the women came out of all the cities of Israel, singing and dancing, to meet King Saul, with tambourines, with joy and with musical instruments. 7 The women sang as they played, and said, "Saul has slain his thousands, And David his ten thousands." 8 Then Saul became very angry, for this saying displeased him; and he said, "They have ascribed to David ten thousands, but to me they have ascribed thousands. Now what more can he have but the kingdom?"

1E - "[9] Saul looked at David with suspicion from that day on. [10] Now it came about on…. *(4,438 more words in full version.)*

Tip #14 - Develop a Conqueror Mentality

1A - God wants each of us to be strong and able to handle any problem that comes our way. A good example of this is the young man David, who found out about a giant named, Goliath, who was making fun of the Israelite army. When the time came, David marched up in great boldness and he defeated the giant!

1B - Here is the account:

1 Samuel 17:20 – 51 "So David arose early in the morning and left the flock with a keeper and took *the supplies* and went as Jesse had commanded him. And he came to the circle of the camp while the army was going out in battle array shouting the war cry. [21] Israel and the Philistines drew up in battle array, army against army. [22] Then David left his baggage in the care of the baggage keeper, and ran to the battle line and entered in order to greet his brothers. [23] As he was talking with them, behold, the champion, the Philistine from Gath named Goliath, was coming up from the army of the Philistines, and he spoke these same words; and David heard *them*."

1C - "[24] When all the men of Israel saw the man, they fled from him and were greatly afraid. [25] The men of Israel said, "Have you seen this man who is coming up? Surely he is coming up to defy Israel. And it will be that the king will enrich the man who kills him with great riches and will give him his daughter and make his father's house free in Israel." [26] Then David spoke to the men who were standing by him, saying, "What will be done for the man who kills this Philistine and takes away the reproach from Israel? For who is this uncircumcised Philistine, that he should taunt the armies of the living God?" [27] The people answered him in accord with this word, saying, "Thus it will be done for the man who kills him."

1D - "Now Eliab his oldest…. *(2,089 more words in full version.)*

Tip #16 - Develop a Disciplined Lifestyle

1A - The essence of discipline is denying ourselves things of low value to gain something of greater value. Few great things in life are accomplished without discipline. Every athlete will tell you it took discipline of diet, exercise and practice to become good at what they do. Every successful business person will tell you it took long hours and hard work to get to where they got in the business world. Discipline is a key ingredient to living a successful life.

Question 1: Can you think of a person who is successful and disciplined? If so, can you tell us in what way they are disciplined?

2A - Bible Verses on Being Disciplined and Self-Controlled

a) **Galatians 5:22-23** "But the fruit of the Spirit is love, joy, peace, patience, kindness, goodness, faithfulness, gentleness, self-control; against such things there is no law."

b) **1 Thessalonians 5:6** "so then let us not sleep as others do, but let us be alert and sober."

c) **Titus 1:8** "but hospitable, loving what is good, sensible, just, devout, self-controlled,"

d) **1 Peter 1:13** "Therefore, prepare your minds for action, keep sober in spirit, fix your hope completely on the grace to be brought to you at the revelation of Jesus Christ."

e) **1 Peter 5:8** "Be of sober spirit, be on the alert. Your adversary, the devil, prowls around like a roaring lion, seeking someone to devour:"

Question 2: Can you recall anyone in your life who taught you to be disciplined? If so, what did they say to you?

3A - Following, are instructions Paul gave to Titus on how Christians should live. Much….. *(929 more words in full version.)*

Tip #17 - Develop a Lifestyle of Holiness

Just as He chose us in Him before the foundation of the world, that we would be holy and blameless before Him. In love. Ephesians 1:4

1A - The central theme of the Bible is to show us how to have a relationship with God and the forgiveness we need through our Lord Jesus Christ. In the Old Testament, we read about God's high standards for daily living. They were so high that no one was able to achieve it. People sinned. The only thing that could pay the penalty for sin was blood. Thus, in the Old Testament God instructed His people to sacrifice animals once a year to pay for the sins of the people.

1B - Then a better sacrifice came, the Lord Jesus Christ. Two thousand years ago, the blood of a sinless man, Jesus Christ, was spilled, to pay the penalty for the sin of all of humanity. It was a horrendous day - but a monumental day, the day Jesus allowed Himself to be nailed to a cross. Because of Jesus, we can trade our sin nature for a new nature. Thank God for Jesus!

1C - Why did Jesus have to die? Why did animals have to die? Because of sin.

If sin is so terrible that it cost the lives of numerous animals, and the life of a perfect human being - Jesus Christ, shouldn't we be living holy lives? Absolutely.

The problem is that living holy lives rarely comes up in people's minds. Most people end up living half-hearted, semi-holy lives. This kind of lifestyle can become a hindrance to our happiness.

1D - We should understand, however, that our motive for living a holy life is not so that we can buy ourselves a place in heaven after we die. The Bible says that our best works are like filthy rags in God's sight (See Isaiah 64:6 below). Our good works could never be good enough to save our souls. We need the.... *(2,,409 more words in full version.)*

Tip #19 - Eliminate Anger

1A - Anger is a definite hindrance to happiness. Many of us have triggers that bring on our anger. It is helpful to take time to assess the root causes of our anger and learn how to disarm it.

In a June 29, 2017 article in Time Magazine entitled, "The Rage Flu - Why All This Anger is Contagious and Making Us Sick, Dr. Gary Slutkin, founder of Cure Violence, and a faculty member of the University of Illinois at Chicago is quoted as saying "Violence and violent speech meet the criteria of disease... Like a virus, violence makes more of itself. Rage begets more rage. And it spreads because we humans are wired to follow our peers."

1B - The author of the magazine article, Susanna Schrobsdorff, adds that "...if extreme speech becomes acceptable in one realm, it's likely to spread to overlapping realms – from the dinner table, to social feeds, to a political demonstration. ...And for the more vulnerable, those who are mentally unstable or disenfranchised, this sickness can lead to actual violence directed at the person or institution that symbolizes their disappointment." Ms. Schrobsdorff also quotes Dr. Slutkin as saying "Undesirable social norms are becoming more prevalent."

1C - Anger and Anxiety

Something to note is that there can be a link between anxiety and anger. If we've never learned how to calm ourselves down, and problems come up, they can trigger an anger response in us. When we see that our anger can "freeze" those around us, we can use it to influence others to do what we want - whenever we want. However, our anger can stop us from developing emotionally.

Question 1: What tends to trigger your anger?

2A - Jesus was very much.... *(1,220 more words in full version.)*

Tip #18 - Become an Optimist

1A - Can you think of someone who is always optimistic? Is that a good way to be? In this Tip, we will learn how optimism relates to the Christian life. The definition of optimism in the Merriam-Webster dictionary is: "The tendency to be hopeful and to emphasize or think of the good part in a situation rather than the bad part, or the feeling that in the future good things are more likely to happen than bad things:"

Question 1: In general, what is your level of optimism?

2A - Below, are some quotes on optimism.

a) "Optimism is the faith that leads to achievement. Nothing can be done without hope and confidence." – Helen Keller

b) "One of the things I learned the hard way was that it doesn't pay to get discouraged. Keeping busy and making optimism a way of life can restore your faith in yourself." – Lucille Ball

c) "Be fanatically positive and militantly optimistic. If something is not to your liking, change your liking." – Rick Steves

d) "A healthy attitude is contagious but don't wait to catch it from others. Be a carrier." – Author Unknown

Question 2: What thoughts come to your mind after reading the above quotes on optimism?

3A - The Book of Galatians give an overview of the character traits of people who follow Christ. Some burst with optimism, others not so readily at first glance. Let's see how they relate.

Galatians 5:22,23 "But the fruit of the Spirit is love, joy, peace, patience, kindness, goodness, faithfulness, gentleness, self-control; against such things there is no law."

3B - Love – An optimistic.... *(2,293 more words in full version.)*

Tip #20 - Practice Humility

1A - Learning to be humble is one of the most attractive attributes we can develop. The word "humble" is defined as having, or showing, a modest or low estimate of one's importance.

We don't have to be lower in importance; rather we give others the privilege of being higher than us.

Jesus taught the paradox, to become great, one must become humble.

a) **Matthew 18:4** "Whoever then humbles himself as this child, he is the greatest in the kingdom of heaven."

b) **Matthew 23:12** "Whoever exalts himself shall be humbled; and whoever humbles himself shall be exalted."

1B - Jesus taught us humility by displaying it in a number of ways.

First, He was born in a humble place, a barn.

Luke 2:16 "So they came in a hurry and found their way to Mary and Joseph, and the baby as He lay in the manger."

1C - Second, He was humble toward His parents.

Luke 2:51 "And He went down with them and came to Nazareth, and He continued in subjection to them; and His mother treasured all these things in her heart."

1D - Third, Jesus never had a house.

Luke 9:58 "And Jesus said to him, "The foxes have holes and the birds of the air have nests, but the Son of Man has nowhere to lay His head.""

1E - Fourth, Jesus spent His teaching days as a servant.

a) **Matthew 20:28** "just as the Son of Man did not come to be served, but to serve, and to give His life a ransom for many."

b) **Luke 22:27** "For who.... *(1,144 more words in full version.)*

Tip #21 - Collect "Grace Doors"

1A - It was Thanksgiving weekend, and a gentleman was waiting his turn to drive out of a grocery store parking lot. To his left, he saw an older woman backing out of her parking spot heading straight for his driver's door. It looked like she wasn't going to stop, so the man honked his horn, but her car kept going and hit his door. The two drivers got out of their vehicles to assess the damage, and to exchange driver's licenses and insurance information. The gentleman could smell alcohol on the breath of the other driver.

1B - About an hour later, the gentleman called the woman driver and told her, "I've decided not to pursue the insurance claim on the dented door. I am a handy person, so repairing the door is not a big deal for me. Plus, I know one day I'm going to make a mistake and will need grace, so I am "paying it forward" by giving you grace for the dented door. I hope you have a nice Thanksgiving weekend."

1C - The woman was speechless. Her husband had to come on the phone to finish the call. The gentleman explained to the husband what he had just told his wife. The husband said his wife was speechless and thanked the man very much for the call.

1D - This example shows what we mean by the term "Grace Door," a situation in which we give someone grace for a mistake they have made.

Question 1: Have you ever given someone grace like this? If so, can you tell us about it?

2A - The truth is, we all make mistakes, and it's only a matter of time before we make our next mistake. Thus, it's good to be prepared for them. One way to be prepared is to have "Grace Doors" in our "account." That means having a number of past instances where we have given grace to people…. (*718 more words in full version.*)

Tip #23 - Conquer the Addiction

1A - Addictions are fast becoming a major problem in our communities, with some areas reaching crisis levels. Therefore the church should be ready to meet the needs of people caught in a cycle of defeat due to addictions.

1B - Any activity we feel compelled to do regularly, to feel better, could be an addiction. We shouldn't be fooled by the low statistics of a behavior. If we need something to dull emotional pain, we should assess the root cause of this urge to see if it is an addiction. Some of the more common addictions are over-eating, alcohol, drugs, pornography, sex, shopping, gambling, video gaming, television, and work. Sadly, addictions are even prevalent in the church. We need God to help us in this regard.

Below are some scriptures related to addiction.

a) **Deuteronomy 21:20** "They shall say to the elders of his city, 'This son of ours is stubborn and rebellious, he will not obey us, he is a glutton and a drunkard.'"

b) **Proverbs 23:21** "For the heavy drinker and the glutton will come to poverty, And drowsiness will clothe one with rags."

c) **Matthew 11:19** "The Son of Man came eating and drinking, and they say, 'Behold, a gluttonous man and a drunkard, a friend of tax collectors and sinners!' Yet wisdom is vindicated by her deeds."

d) **Luke 7:34** "The Son of Man has come eating and drinking, and you say, 'Behold, a gluttonous man and a drunkard, a friend of tax collectors and sinners!'"

Question 1: What addictions do people, you know, struggle with today?

2A - Reasons to Break an Addiction (*2,080 more words in full version.*)

Tip #22 - Volunteer

1A - When our day-to-day life becomes a constant struggle, it can be tempting to just stay home and do nothing. However, great blessings await us if we will move out of our comfort zone and help make a difference in other people's lives. A great way to do this is through volunteering. Real benefits can be had, even if we only volunteer for an hour a week.

1B - It can be surprising how God uses our volunteering to direct us to new people who can enrich our lives. He can also use our past experiences to help us to do a good job in a volunteer position. Volunteering has a way of expanding our vision to new ideas we could never have come up with otherwise. Here's how volunteering can help us.

a) Volunteering can help take our mind off whatever is bothering us.

b) Volunteering helps us network with others.

c) Volunteering can lead to promotions.

d) Volunteering can advance our career.

e) Volunteering can help us live a more active lifestyle.

f) Volunteering can add a sense of fun and excitement to our lives.

Question 1: Can you tell us in what ways you've volunteered in the past? If so, how did it help you?

2A - A Good Distraction

Volunteering can help distract us from thinking negatively. This is a huge benefit for people who struggle with anxiety or depression. Choosing a volunteer position that entails meeting new people and learning new skills helps…. (*2,381 more words in full version.*)

Tip #24 - Have a Vision for Your Life

1A - God has created us for a purpose. The Bible says He laid out the purpose for our lives before we were even born. **Ephesians 2:10** says, "For we are His workmanship, created in Christ Jesus for good works, which God prepared beforehand so that we would walk in them."

Our life's purpose will eventually begin manifesting at some point in our life. We call this birthing stage of a mission, a vision. It is a captivating, irresistible sense of something we must do. It can come suddenly, or it can happen slowly, over days, weeks, and months. The following scripture gives us a sense of the importance of a vision.

Proverbs 29:18 "Where there is no vision, the people are unrestrained, But happy is he who keeps the law."

Question 1: Have you ever had a vision or a sense of what you were supposed to do?

2A - Begin with a Prayer

Life can have a way of "knocking the wind out of us." The challenges of life can sometimes seem impossible to conquer, and we are tempted to adopt a defeatist attitude. But just because one door of opportunity closes on us, doesn't mean new doors can't open. If a dream we've been holding on to falls apart, we can ask God for a new purpose for our life, and He will give it to us. Here is a well known Bible verse on getting guidance. We can use it to help steer us to our next vision, or goal, in life.

Proverbs 3:5-6 "Trust in the Lord with all your heart And do not lean on your own understanding. In all your ways acknowledge Him, And He will make your paths straight."

Question 2: Have you ever felt like you couldn't go any further? If so, would you like to share with us what happened?

3A - Become Unstoppable! (*1,232 more words in full version.*)

Tip #25 - Be Thankful

1A - Another helpful attribute to develop in our lives is that of being thankful. Scientific research shows that thankfulness boosts the immune system and increases blood supply, both of which contribute to improved physical and emotional health. Research also shows that it enhances alertness, enthusiasm, energy, and sleep improvements. All of these benefits contribute to less stress, anxiety, and depression.

The Bible refers to thanksgiving many times. Below are some of the key verses for gratitude.

Question 1: How would you rate your level of thankfulness?

2A - Below is a verse that tells us to be thankful for all things. Does the Apostle Paul mean for us to be thank for bad things that happen to us, as well? Good question.

Ephesians 5:20 "always giving thanks for all things in the name of our Lord Jesus Christ to God, even the Father;"

Below is a verse that tells us to be thankful "in" all things. This is something we can definitely do, if not the above.

1 Thessalonians 5:18 "in everything give thanks; for this is God's will for you in Christ Jesus."

Question 2: Can you think of a time when you were thankful "for" or "in" a negative event in your life?

3A - A Good Reason To Be Thankful – God's Mercy

The Bible doesn't just say "give thanks," sometimes it says "O give thanks."

a) Psalms 106:1 "Praise the Lord! Oh give thanks to the Lord, for He is good; For His lovingkindness is everlasting."

b) Psalms 118:1 "Give…. (*832 more words in full version.*)

Tip #27 - Resolve Delayed Maturity

"When I was a child, I used to speak like a child, think like a child, reason like a child; when I became a man, I did away with childish things." 1 Corinthians 13:11

1A - It is important for us to attain maturity in all aspects of our life. This is because we influence those around us. If people see us engage in certain behaviors, they will consider doing them as well. Thus it is essential to model maturity - emotionally, intellectually, behaviorally and spiritually. A healthy, thriving society depends on it.

1B - Who is This Tip For?

This Tip is primarily written for young people. Knowing vital information when we are young means we won't have to struggle through some pitfalls that catch young people off guard in today's society. This Tip will also alert us to weaknesses we may not know we have. Knowing our weaknesses, early in life, means we can guard them and work on them before they develop into unmanageable problems later in life.

Finally, knowing what a well-adjusted life looks like, early on, will better prepare us to raise our children successfully when that time comes.

Question 1: Can you think of any young people who are presently struggling in life?

2A - Delayed Maturity

Sometimes unhappiness is linked to areas of our lives that are not fully matured. Delayed maturity can come from early childhood trauma. It can also come from an unhealthy home environment growing up. Thirdly, it can from people we associate with during our adolescent and young adult years….. (*3,166 more words in full version.*)

Tip #26 - Welcome MLCs

1A - Life can be filled with challenges. Thus, it is good to be prepared when these challenges come around. One way to be prepared is to be able to welcome MLC's. "MLC" stands for Major Life Challenge. They are the more difficult times in our lives such as the death of a loved one, spouse wanting a divorce, negative diagnosis, job loss, serious injury, relocation, lawsuit, and financial loss. Each of these requires an adjustment in our thinking so we keep our peace of mind.

Question 1: Can you think of a time in your life when you were faced with an MLC? If so, how well did you handle it?

2A - Why "Welcome" MLCs?

At first glance, we might wonder why we would want to welcome one of these events in our lives. We will examine the reasons below.

First, as Christians, God requires us to live by faith. That means that we trust God in every aspect of our lives; this includes the difficult times. Our faith tells us that God can heal a negative situation, or bring good out of it.

a) Romans 1:17 "But the righteous man shall live by faith." (Also found in Habakkuk 2:4, Galatians 3:11 and Hebrews 10:38.)

b) 2 Corinthians 12:9 "And He has said to me, "My grace is sufficient for you, for power…. (*2,185 more words in full version.*)

Tip #28 - Sing

1A - According to a number of sources*, singing can help us overcome anxiety and depression. One such write-up is the August 16, 2013, Time Magazine article entitled, "Singing Changes Your Brain." See quotes below.

"When you sing, musical vibrations move through you, altering your physical and emotional landscape. Group singing, for those who have done it, is the most exhilarating and transformative of all. It takes something incredibly intimate, a sound that begins inside you, shares it with a roomful of people and it comes back as something even more thrilling: harmony."

1B - The article goes on to say, "The elation may come from endorphins, a hormone released by singing, which is associated with feelings of pleasure. Or it might be from oxytocin, another hormone released during singing, which has been found to alleviate anxiety and stress. Oxytocin also enhances feelings of trust and bonding, which may explain why still more studies have found that singing lessens feelings of depression and loneliness."…. (*2,945 more words in full version.*)

Tip #29 - Join a Church

1A - In this Tip, we are going to see that the Christian church is the center of the community. We will also look at the purpose of the church, part of which, is to show us how to live above anxiety and depression.

Not every congregation meets in a public building, but wherever a church meets, that is the focus of all of heaven. See below.

Hebrews 12:1 "Therefore, since we have so great a cloud of witnesses surrounding us, let us also lay aside every encumbrance and the sin which so easily entangles us, and let us run with endurance the race that is set before us,"

Thus, heaven has the greatest "reality show" in the universe. They are watching us GO!

1B - How the Church Got Started

After God, the Father, resurrected Jesus from the dead, Jesus commissioned His disciples to go and preach the Gospel of forgiveness through Christ Jesus throughout…. (*5,529 more words in full version.*)

Affirmation #1
"I Do Not Fear"

Throughout your day, try to recite out loud, the "I Do Not Fear" Affirmation.

Prayer of Dedication: "Father, I dedicate myself to live a life free of all fear. I now speak these Bible-based statements out loud to build in me a rock solid faith that keeps me at peace all day long."

1) It is the Lord, who goes before me, He is with me, He will not leave me, nor fail me. I do not fear, nor am I dismayed. Based on Deuteronomy 31:8.

2) No one is able, to stand before me, all the days of my life. As God was with Moses, He is with me; He will never fail me, nor forsake me. Based on Joshua 1:5.

3) I am strong, and courageous, I am careful to obey, all the laws of God, I do not turn from it, to the right, or to the left, and I succeed, wherever I go. Based on Joshua 1:7.

4) I am strong, and courageous. I do not tremble, nor am I dismayed, for the Lord my God, is with me, wherever I go. Based on Joshua 1:9.

5) I listen to God, and I live securely, I am at ease, from the dread of evil. Based on Proverbs 1:33.

6) I walk in my way, securely, my foot does not stumble. Based on Proverbs 3:23.

7) When I lie down, I will not be afraid, when I lie down, my sleep is sweet. Based on Proverbs 3:24.

8) I am not afraid, of sudden fear, nor the onslaught, of the wicked, when they come, the Lord is my confidence, He keeps my foot, from being caught. Based on Proverbs 3:25-26.

9) The fear of man, brings a snare, but because I trust in the Lord, I am exalted. Based on Proverbs 29:25.

10) The Lord is a shield for me, He lifts up my head. Based on Psalm 3:3.

11) I lie down and sleep. I wake again, because the Lord sustains me. Based on Psalm 3:5.

12) I am not afraid, of tens of thousands of people, who have set themselves against me, all around. Based on Psalm 3:6.

13) When evil doers come up against me, they stumble and fall. Based on Psalm 27:2.

14) The LORD is my light, and my salvation, whom shall I fear? The Lord is the defense of my life, of whom shall I dread? Based on Psalm 27:1.

15) Though a host encamps against me, my heart will not fear; though war rises against me, I am confident. Based on Psalm 27:3.

16) For in my time of trouble, He conceals me in His tabernacle; In the secret place, of His tent, He hides me. He lifts me up, on a rock. Based on Psalm 27:5.

17) My head is lifted up, above the enemies, all around me; In His tent, I offer shouts of joy; I sing praises to the LORD. Based on Psalm 27:6.

18) Though my father and mother, forsake me, the LORD will take me up. Based on Psalm 27:10.

19) I wait for the LORD; I am strong, and my heart takes courage, I wait for the LORD. Based on Psalm 27:14.

20) I sought the Lord, and He answered me, and delivered me, from all my fears. Based on Psalm 34:4.

21) I stop myself, from being angry, I forsake my wrath, I do not fret, for any reason. Based on Psalm 37:8.

(30 other statements in full program)

Affirmation #2
"I Am Strong"

Throughout your day, try to recite out loud, the "I Am Strong" Affirmation.

Prayer of Dedication: "Father, I dedicate myself to live this day with a 'strength conscious' mindset. I now speak these Bible-based statements out loud to build in me a strong spirit that carries me victoriously through each challenge in my day!"

1) No man is able, to stand before me, all the days of my life, as God was with Moses, He is with me, my God will not leave me, nor forsake me, I am strong, I have good courage. Based on Joshua 1:5.

2) For by God, I can run upon a troop, and leap over a wall, Based on 2 Samuel 22:30.

3) God's Word is proven, He is a shield to me, because I trust Him. Based on 2 Samuel 22:31.

4) God is my rock, and my fortress, and my deliverer; my God my strength, in whom I take refuge; He is my shield, the horn of my salvation, my stronghold. Based on Psalm 18:2.

5) God arms me with strength, He makes my way blameless, He makes my feet, like hinds' feet, He sets me on high places, God trains my hands for battle, so that my arms, can bend a bow of bronze. Based on Psalm 18:32-34.

6) I pursue my enemies, I overtaken them, I do not turn back, until they are consumed, I shatter them, so they cannot rise, they fall under my feet. Based on Psalm 18:37,38.

7) God has armed me, with strength for battle, God subdues those under me, those who rise up against me. Based on Psalm 18:39.

8) I wait on the Lord; I am strong, and my heart takes courage, I wait on the Lord. Based on Psalm 27:14.

9) The Lord is my strength, and my shield, My heart trusts in Him. Based on Psalm 28:7.

10) Because of Your favor, upon my life, You have made my mountain, to stand strong. Based on Psalm 30:7.

11) I am strong, and my heart takes courage, I strengthen my heart, as I hope in the Lord. Based on Psalm 31:24.

12) There is no reason, for me to despair, or be disturbed. My hope is in God. And I praise Him, He helps my countenance shine, He is my God. Based on Psalm 42:11.

13) Through God, I push back my adversaries, Through God's name, I trample those, who rise up against me. Based on Psalm 44:5.

14) God is in the midst of me, I will not be moved: God helps me, when the morning dawns. Based on Psalm 46:5.

15) God is my salvation, and my glory, the rock of my strength, My refuge is in God. Based on Psalm 62:7.

16) I proclaim good news; Kings of armies flee. I remain, and I divide the spoil! Based on Psalms 68:11,12.

17) God is the strength, of my heart, forever. Based on Psalm 73:26.

18) I dwell in the shelter, of the Most High, and I abide in the shadow, of the Almighty. Based on Psalm 91:1.

19) I flourish like a palm tree, I grow like a cedar, in Lebanon, I am planted, in the house of the Lord, and I flourish, in the courts of my God. Based on Psalm 92:12 & 13.

20) God satisfies my mouth, with good things; so that my youth, is renewed like the eagles. Based on Psalm 103:5.

(30 other statements in full program)

Affirmation #3
"I Flow In Harmony and Love"

Throughout your day, try to recite out loud, the "I Flow in Harmony and Love" Affirmation.

Prayer of Dedication: "Father, I dedicate myself to live this day with a love saturated mindset. I now speak these Bible-based statements out loud, to build in me a heart of love that is present in everything I think, say, and do."

1) I am careful to remove the "log," out of my own eye, before trying to remove the speck, out of my brothers (or sisters) eye. Based on Matthew 7:5.

2) When Jesus saw the crowd, He had compassion on them. I too have compassion, on all who are in my life. Based on Matthew 9:36.

3) I work hard, to support the week, I remember the words, of the Lord Jesus, it is more blessed to give, than to receive. Jesus is making me, into a very compassionate, giving person. Based on Acts 20:35.

4) I do not think of myself, more highly than I ought, but to have sound judgment, allowing others to have importance too. Based on Romans 12:3.

5) I am devoted to others, with brotherly love; I give preference to others, I give them honor. Based on Romans 12:10.

6) I contribute, to the needs, of the saints, I practice hospitality. Based on Romans 12:13.

7) I do not repay evil for evil, I respect what is right, in the sight of all men. Based on Romans 12:17.

8) I am not overcome by evil, I overcome evil with good. Based on Romans 12:21.

9) I love my neighbor as myself. I never do wrong to my neighbor. When I love, I am fulfilling the law. Based on Romans 13:9,10.

10) I behave properly, as in the day, never carousing, and drunkenness, never in sexual promiscuity and sensuality, nor in strife, or jealousy. Based on Romans 13:13.

11) I pursue things, which make for peace, and the building up of others. Based on Romans 14:19.

12) I please my neighbor, for His good, for His edification. Based on Romans 15:2.

13) God who gives me perseverance and encouragement, helps me to be likeminded, with other people, according to Christ Jesus. Based on Romans 15:5.

14) Father, your love, has been shed abroad, in my heart, by the Holy Spirit, I therefore patient, I am kind, I am not jealous, I do not brag, and am not arrogant. Based on 1 Corinthians 13:4.

15) I do not act unbecomingly. I do not seek my own way. I am not provoked. I do not take into account a suffered wrong. Based on 1 Corinthians. 13:5.

16) I do not rejoice in unrighteousness, I rejoice in the truth. Based on 1 Corinthians 13:6.

17) I bear up under all things, I believe the best about people.

18) My love never fails. Based on 1 Corinthians 13:8.

19) I pursue love. And I desire spiritual gifts. Based on 1 Corinthians 14:1.

20) When I see a brother or sister, caught in a trespass, I restore such a person, in a spirit of gentleness. Based on Galatians 6:1.

21) With all humility and gentleness, and with patience, I show tolerance toward others, in love. Based on Ephesians 4:2.

22) I am diligent, to preserve, the unity of the Spirit, with others, in the bond of peace. Based on Ephesians 4:3.

(5 other statements in full program)

Affirmation #4
"I Only Speak Right Words"

Throughout your day, try to recite out loud, the "I Only Speak Right Words" Affirmation.

Prayer of Dedication: "Father, I dedicate myself to live this day speaking only right words, words that are free of all negatives. I now speak these Bible-based statements out loud to remind me to keep all my words positive and faith-filled!"

1) My words are as a honeycomb, sweet to the soul, and healing to the bones. Based on Psalm 16:24.

2) My words are like a wellspring of wisdom, and as a flowing brook. Based on Proverbs18:4.

3) Because I guard my mouth, and my tongue, I guard my soul from troubles. Based on Proverbs 21:23.

4) Because I am righteous, my mouth speaks wisdom, and my tongue speaks what is just. Based on Psalm 37:30.

5) My heart thinks of good things. I speak things that help others. My words are like those, of a ready writer, recording good things. Based on Psalm 45:1.

6) I put away from me, a deceitful mouth, and devious speech, I put far from me. Based on Proverbs 4:24.

7) I speak God's Words, because they are life to me, they are health, to all my body. Based on Proverbs 4:22.

8) All the words of my mouth, are in righteousness; there is nothing crooked, or perverted in them. Based on Proverbs 8:8.

9) I speak noble things, and the opening of my lips, reveal right things only. My mouth speaks truth, and wickedness, is an abomination to my words. Based on Proverbs 8:6,7.

10) I have the mouth, of a righteous man, my words are like a fountain of life. Based on Proverbs 10:11.

11) Because I am righteous, my words are like choice silver. Based on Proverbs 10:20.

12) Because I am righteous, my words feed many. Based on Proverbs 10:21.

13) Because I am righteous, the words of my mouth bring forth wisdom, continually. Based on Proverbs 10:31.

14) Because I am righteous, my lips know, what is acceptable. Based on Proverbs 10:32.

15) I am satisfied with good, by the fruit of my words. Based on Proverbs 12:14.

16) Because I have God's wisdom, my words bring healing. Based on Proverbs 12:18.

17) Because I guard my words, I preserve my life, He that talks too much invites ruin into his life. Therefore, I watch what I say. Based on Proverbs 13:3.

18) Because a harsh word stirs up anger, I answer people gently, and my gentle answers turn away wrath. Based on Proverbs 15:1.

19) Because I continually seek knowledge, my wisdom helps me speak what is acceptable. The mouth of fools spout foolishness. Based on Proverbs 15:2.

20) My soothing words produce a tree of life. Based on Proverbs 15:4.

21) I have joy, when I answer properly. My timely words produce delight! Based on Proverbs 15:23.

22) As I prepare my heart, each day with prayer, and the Word, I believe the answers, of my tongue, are from the Lord. Based on Proverbs 16:1.

(2 other statements in full program)

Affirmation #5

"I Only Think Right Thoughts"

Throughout your day, try to recite out loud, the "I Only Think Right Thoughts" Affirmation.

Prayer of Dedication: "Father, I dedicate myself to live this day thinking only right thoughts, thoughts that are free of all negatives. I now speak these Bible-based statements out loud to remind me to keep all my thoughts positive and faith-filled!"

1) I trust in the Lord, with all my heart, and I do not lean, on my own understanding. In all my ways, I acknowledge Him, and He makes my paths straight. Based on Proverbs 3:5-6.

2) I meditate, on God's Word, day and night, I am like a tree, planted by streams, that yeilds forth its fruit, in season. And my leaves, do not wither, in whatever I do, I prosper. Based on Psalm 1:2-3.

3) I pray every day, for God's help, to keep the words of my mouth, and the meditation of my heart, acceptable, in His sight. Based on Psalm 19:14.

4) I thank God, that he leads me (and my thoughts), beside quiet waters, and he restores my soul, with good thoughts, and he leads me, in paths of righteousness, for His name's sake. Based on Psalm 23:2,3.

5) I am diligent, to treasure God's Word, in my heart, so that I, may not sin, against Him. Based on Psalm 119:11.

6) I ask God, to search me every day, to know my heart, and try my thoughts, to see if there is, any anxious thoughts in me, and if there is any hurtful way in me, And to lead me, in the everlasting way. Based on Psalm 139:23,24.

7) I watch over my heart, (my thoughts), with all diligence, for out of it, flow the springs of my life. Based on Proverbs 4:23.

8) I bring to God, the plans in my mind, and he helps me, to know which way to go. (This keeps my mind at rest.) Based on Proverbs 16:3.

9) My joyful heart, is good medicine. (So I keep myself happy, hopeful, and trusting in God.) Based on Proverbs 17:22.

10) Because I keep my mind, steadfast on God, He helps me have perfect peace. Based on Isaiah 26:3.

11) I forsake my old deeds and thoughts, and I return to the Lord, He has compassion on me, and He abundantly pardons me. Based on Isaiah 55:7.

12) I keep myself hopeful, because God has plans for my welfare, He has plans to give me, a future and a hope. Based on Jeremiah 29:11.

13) I am diligent, to love God, with all my heart, with all my soul, with all my mind. Based on Matthew 22:37.

14) Jesus left His peace with me, Jesus gave me His peace. I stop my heart, from being troubled, I never let it be fearful. Based on John 14:27.

15) Because I live after the Spirit, I mind the things of the Spirit, and not the flesh. Based on Romans 8:5.

16) I do not let myself, be conformed, to this world, but I allow myself, to be transformed, by the renewing of my mind. This way I am able to know the good, the acceptable, and the perfect will of God, for my life. Based on Romans 12:2.

17) The weapons that God has given me, are not fleshly, but divinely powered for the destruction of fortresses, in my mind. I destroy speculations, and every lofty thing, that rises up, against the knowledge of God, and I take, every thought captive, to the obedience of Christ. Based on 2 Corinthians 10:4,5.

18) As a person thinks, so are they. (And because I am a Christian, saved by the sacrifice of Jesus, I have been Born Again. I am a new creature in Christ Jesus. I have traded my sin nature, for....

(12 other statements in full program)

Affirmation #6

"I am Happy Because.."

Throughout your day, try to recite out loud, the "I Am Happy Because..." Affirmation.

Prayer of Dedication: "Father, I dedicate myself to live this day rejoicing in the things you have given me. I now speak these Bible-based statements to remind me of all the good things I have because I am your child!"

1) I am happy because, those who mourn, will be comforted! Based on Matthew 5:4.

2) I am happy because, I know how to glorify God, by letting my light shine, before men, by doing good works. Based on Matthew 5:16.

3) I am happy because, I don't have to have negative feelings, about my enemies, I love them, and I pray for them. Based on Matthew 5:44.

4) I am happy because, when I give, and pray, and fast, in secret, God rewards me openly. Based on Matthew 6:4,6.

5) I am happy because, all my needs are met, when I seek first God's kingdom, and His righteousness. Based on Matthew 6:33, Luke 12:31.

6) I am happy because, when I ask - I receive, when I seek - I find, when I knock - it is opened. Based on Matthew 7:7, Luke 11:10.

7) I am happy because, when I labor, and am heavy laden, Jesus bids me come, he gives me rest! Based on Matthew 11:28,29.

8) I am happy because, even a small amount of faith, can do so much. Based on Matthew 17:20.

9) I am happy because, when two people agree, in prayer, it will be done, by my Father in heaven. Based on Matthew 18:19.

10) I am happy because, where 2 or 3 believers are, Christ is in the midst. Based on Matthew 18:20.

11) I am happy because, all things are possible! Based on Matthew 19:26 & Mark 9:23.

12) I am happy because, when I give to the needy, I give to Christ! Based on Matthew 25:40.

13) I am happy because, Jesus can take, what little I have, and multiply it! Based on Mark 8:1-9.

14) I am happy because, Jesus lays out an easy way, to become great – become a servant of all! Based on Mark 9:35, 10:4

15) I am happy because, Jesus said, whatever I pray for, and believe I have received it, I shall have it! Based on Mark 11:24.

16) I am happy because, I don't have to worry, about saying the wrong things, Jesus said the Holy Ghost, will give me the words to say. Based on Mark 13:11.

17) I am happy because, Jesus doesn't care how little, my offering is, it's how much is left over that counts! Based on Mark 12:43,44.

18) I am happy because, God gives me purpose! Jesus tells me to "Go into all the world, and preach the gospel, to all creation." That's my purpose! Based on Mark 16:15.

19) I am happy because, whoever believes, and is baptized, will be saved! Based on Mark 16:16.

20) I am happy because, Jesus said we can heal people, in His name! Based on Mark 16:18.

21) I am happy because, Jesus said those who weep now, will one day laugh! Based on Luke 6:21.

22) I am happy because, I don't have to care, when people dislike me, Jesus said to rejoice, for my reward, in heaven, will be great! Based on Luke 6:22,23.

(137 other statements in full program)

Core Beliefs

Choose Your Core Beliefs

Our thoughts are influenced by our beliefs. Positive beliefs help keep our thinking and our responses to life's problems positive.

The goal is to make these core beliefs the final word in our lives. No matter what our feelings say or what the circumstances try to tell us, these foundational beliefs are what we are going to use when thinking about ourselves, when making decisions in our lives, and when we are praying about our needs and wants.

If we come across a belief that we would like to adopt but seems untrue to us, read out loud the scripture verses associated with the belief. The truth of these verses will slowly sink into our minds and over time will become real in our hearts.

****

Core Belief #1

"Based on the following scriptures, I believe God loves me, and that I am valuable."

Below are some scriptures that talk about God's love for humanity. The most notable way God showed His love for us is in the offering of His only Son, Jesus, to die on the cross for our sins. Indeed, His love for us is great.

Remember that this is a Core Belief. Unless we believe this to be true, our lives can seem meaningless and hopeless. So let's renew our minds to the truth that God loves us, and that He has an amazing plan for our lives!

1) **Nehemiah 9:17** "But You are a God of forgiveness, Gracious and compassionate, Slow to anger and abounding in lovingkindness; And You did not forsake them."

2) **Psalm 17:7** "Wondrously show Your lovingkindness, O Savior of those who take refuge at Your right hand From those who rise up against them."

3) **Psalm 25:7** "Do not remember the sins of my youth or my transgressions; According to Your lovingkindness remember me, For Your goodness' sake, O Lord."

4) **Psalm 36:7** "How precious is Your lovingkindness, O God! And the children of men take refuge in the shadow of Your wings."

5) **Psalm 48:9** "We have thought on Your lovingkindness, O God, In the midst of Your temple."….*(48 other verses in full program).*

Core Belief #2

"Based on the following scriptures, I believe Christ's crucifixion on the cross has paid the penalty for my sin, and that I am destined to live eternally with Christ."

Unless we are convinced that our sins are forgiven, we'll never reach full happiness. If need be, we can read out loud the following scriptures to renew our minds to adopt this vital Core Belief.

1) **John 3:16** "For God so loved the world, that He gave His only begotten Son, that whoever believes in Him shall not perish, but have eternal life."

2) **John 3:17** "For God did not send the Son into the world to judge the world, but that the world might be saved through Him."

3) **Acts 13:38** "Therefore let it be known to you, brethren, that through Him forgiveness of sins is proclaimed to you,"

4) **Acts 13:39** "and through Him everyone who believes is freed from all things, from which you could not be freed through the Law of Moses.

5) **Acts 15:11** "1 But we believe that we are saved through the grace of the Lord Jesus, in the same way as they also are."

6) **Acts 16:30,31** "and after he brought them out, he said, "Sirs, what must I do to be saved?" They said, "Believe in the Lord Jesus, and you will be saved, you and your household.

7) **Romans 1:16** "For I am not ashamed of the gospel, for it is the power of God for salvation to everyone who believes, to the Jew first and also to the Greek."

8) **Romans 3:22-24** "even the righteousness of God through faith in Jesus Christ for all those who believe; for there is no distinction; for all have sinned and fall short of the glory of God, being justified as a gift by His grace through the redemption which is in Christ Jesus;"

9) **Romans 3:25** "whom God displayed publicly as a propitiation in His blood through faith. This was to demonstrate His righteousness, because in the forbearance of God He passed over the sins previously committed;"

10) **Romans 5:1** "Therefore, having been justified by faith, have peace with God through our Lord Jesus Christ,"

11) **Romans 10:4**" For Christ is the end of the law for righteousness to everyone who believes."…. *(51 other verses in full program).*

Core Belief #3

"Based on the following scriptures, I believe God wants me to enjoy perfect peace at all times."

If we don't believe this Core Belief, we'll always wonder when it is OK to be nervous. It's best to believe that peace is always available. And we overcome anything that tries to rob us of God's peace. The peace God gives us passes all understanding (Philippians 4:7) and should never be given up.

1) **Numbers 6:26** "The Lord lift up His countenance on you, And give you peace.'"

2) **Psalm 4:8** "In peace I will both lie down and sleep, For You alone, O Lord, make me to dwell in safety."

3) **Psalm 16:8** "I have set the Lord continually before me; Because He is at my right hand, I will not be shaken."

4) **Psalm 23:1-3** "The Lord is my shepherd, I shall not want. He makes me lie down in green pastures; He leads me beside quiet waters. He restores my soul; He guides me in the paths of righteousness For His name's sake."

5) **Psalm 27:1** "The Lord is my light and my salvation; Whom shall I fear? The Lord is the defense of my life; Whom shall I dread?"

6) **Psalm 29:11** "The Lord will give strength to His people; The Lord will bless His people with peace."

7) **Psalm 37:11** "But the humble will inherit the land And will delight themselves in abundant prosperity."

8) **Psalm 37:37** "Mark the blameless man, and behold the upright; For the man of peace will have a posterity."

9) **Psalm 85:8** "I will hear what God the Lord will say; For He will speak peace to His people, to His godly ones; But let them not turn back to folly."

10) **Psalm 91:1** "He who dwells in the shelter of the Most High, Will abide in the shadow of the Almighty."

11) **Psalm 94:13** "That You may grant him relief from the days of adversity, Until a pit is dug for the wicked."

12) **Psalm 125:1** "Those who trust in the Lord Are as Mount Zion, which cannot be moved but abides forever."

13) **Proverbs 1:33** "But he who listens to me shall live securely And will be at ease from the dread of evil."

14) **Proverbs 3:17** "Her ways are pleasant ways And all her paths are peace."

15) **Proverbs 3:23-24** "Then you will walk in your way securely And your foot will not stumble. When you lie

16) *Isaiah 26:3* "The steadfast of mind You will keep in perfect peace, Because he trusts in You."….. *(51 verses in full program).*

Core Belief #4

"Based on the following scriptures, I believe I have an enemy - Satan."

In 1 Timothy 6:12, we read, "Fight the good fight of faith..." Here we see the Christian life is a battle, a continuous fight for our faith. If we keep our faith intact, then our minds are kept at rest. If we succumb to the plots of our enemy, Satan, who seeks to undermine our faith, then we lose the peace and happiness God has for us, and life becomes difficult. You may not have faith in God at this time; in that case, the enemy will try to steal your faith in yourself. He knows if he can take your self-confidence, he can pull you down in every other aspect of your life. So beware of your enemy! Here are some other scriptures that support this belief that we have an enemy - Satan.

1) **Genesis 3:1** "Now the serpent was more crafty than any beast of the field which the Lord God had made. And he said to the woman, "Indeed, has God said, 'You shall not eat from any tree of the garden'?"
2) **Genesis. 3:4,5** "The serpent said to the woman, "You surely will not die! For God knows that in the day you eat from it your eyes will be opened, and you will be like God, knowing good and evil."
3) **Genesis 3:14** "The Lord God said to the serpent, "Because you have done this, Cursed are you more than all cattle, And more than every beast of the field; On your belly you will go, And dust you will eat All the days of your life;"
4) **Deuteronomy. 32:17** "They sacrificed to demons who were not God, To gods whom they have not known, New gods who came lately, Whom your fathers did not dread."
5) **Job 1:6** "Now there was a day when the sons of God came to present themselves before the Lord, and Satan also came among them."
6) **Job 2:3-7** "The Lord said to Satan, "Have you considered My servant Job? For there is no one like him on the earth, a blameless and upright man fearing God and turning away from evil. And he still holds fast his integrity, although you incited Me against him to ruin him without cause." 4 Satan answered the Lord and said, "Skin for skin! Yes, all that a man has he will give for his life. 5 However, put forth Your hand now, and touch his bone and his flesh; he will curse You to Your face." 6 So the Lord said to Satan, "Behold, he is in your power, only spare his life."
7) **1 Chronicles 21:1** "Then Satan stood up against Israel and moved David to number Israel."… *(72 other verses in full program).*

Core Belief #5

"Based on the following scriptures, I believe I have another enemy - my fleshly appetites."

In 1 Timothy 6:12, we read, "Fight the good fight of faith...". Here we see that the Christian life is a battle, a continuous fight for our faith. If we keep our faith intact, our minds are kept at rest. If we succumb to the plots of our enemy, Satan, to undermine our faith, then we lose the peace and happiness God has for us, and life becomes difficult. Another enemy of the Christian can be the fleshly appetites of the physical body. They can crave things that are not good and can be a distraction taking our focus off of Christ and His plan for our lives. Allowing our fleshly appetites to have their way negatively in our lives will lead us toward anxiety and defeat.

1) **Romans 6:13** "and do not go on presenting the members of your body to sin as instruments of unrighteousness; but present yourselves to God as those alive from the dead, and your members as instruments of righteousness to God."
2) **Romans 7:5** "For while we were in the flesh, the sinful passions, which were aroused by the Law, were at work in the members of our body to bear fruit for death."
3) **Romans 7:18** "For I know that nothing good dwells in me, that is, in my flesh; for the willing is present in me, but the doing of the good is not."

4) **Romans 8:1,2** "Therefore there is now no condemnation for those who are in Christ Jesus. For the law of the Spirit of life in Christ Jesus has set you free from the law of sin and of death."
5) **Romans 8:3** "For what the Law could not do, weak as it was through the flesh, God did: sending His own Son in the likeness of sinful flesh and as an offering for sin, He condemned sin in the flesh,"
6) **Romans 8:4** "so that the requirement of the Law might be fulfilled in us, who do not walk according to the flesh but according to the Spirit"
7) **Romans 8:5** "For those who are according to the flesh set their minds on the things of the flesh, but those who are according to the Spirit, the things of the Spirit."
8) **Romans 8:8** "and those who are in the flesh cannot please God."
9) **Romans 8:9** "However, you are not in the flesh but in the Spirit, if indeed the Spirit of God dwells in you. But if anyone does not have the Spirit of Christ, he does not belong to Him."
10) **Romans 8:10,11** "If Christ is in you, though the body is dead because of sin, yet the spirit is alive because of righteousness. But if the Spirit of Him who raised Jesus from the dead dwells in you, He who raised Christ Jesus from the dead will also give life to your mortal bodies through His Spirit who dwells in you."
11) **Romans 8:12** "So then, brethren, we are under obligation, not to the flesh, to live according….." *(10 other verses in full program).*

Core Belief #6

"Based on the following scriptures, I believe God wants me to enjoy good physical health."

This belief can be difficult to adopt because so many people who pray for healing don't get healed. This is a mystery. However, we know that God responds to faith. Whenever Jesus healed someone, the scriptures say or imply that Jesus marveled at the person's faith. That is what we want Jesus to observe in us; we want Him to marvel at our faith. Thus, the purpose of saying these verses is to help keep our faith strong while we wait for God to move in our situation. As a side-benefit, we will enjoy peace of mind while we wait.

1) **Exodus 15:26** "And He said, "If you will give earnest heed to the voice of the Lord your God, and do what is right in His sight, and give ear to His commandments, and keep all His statutes, I will put none of the diseases on you which I have put on the Egyptians; for I, the Lord, am your healer."
2) **Psalm 30:2** "O Lord my God, I cried to You for help, and You healed me."
3) **Psalm 103:3** "Who pardons all your iniquities, Who heals all your diseases;"
4) **Psalm 107:20** "He sent His word and healed them, And delivered them from their destructions."
5) **Proverbs 3:8** "It will be healing to your body And refreshment to your bones."
6) **Proverbs 4:20-22** "My son, give attention to my words; Incline your ear to my sayings. 21 Do not let them depart from your sight; Keep them in the midst of your heart. 22 For they are life to those who find them And health to all their body."
7) **Proverbs 10:27** "The fear of the Lord prolongs life, But the years of the wicked will be shortened."
8) **Isaiah 53:4-5** "Surely our griefs He Himself bore, And our sorrows He carried; Yet we ourselves esteemed Him stricken, Smitten of God, and afflicted. But He was pierced through for our transgressions, He was crushed for our iniquities; The chastening for our well-being fell upon Him, And by His scourging we are healed."
9) **Jeremiah 17:14** "Heal me, O Lord, and I will be healed; Save me and I will be saved, For You are my praise."
10) **Jeremiah 30:17** "'For I will restore you to health And I will heal you of your wounds,' declares the Lord, 'Because they have called you an outcast, saying:….." *(39 other verses in full program).*

Types of Abuse

When most people hear the word "abuse" they usually think of something very extreme, such as punching or kicking. However, abuse can take non-physical forms too. The following is a list of 6 types of abuse.

Physical
- Any unwanted physical contact
- Kicking, punching
- Pulling, pushing
- Slapping, hitting
- Pulling hair
- Arm twisting
- Holding against wall
- Squeezing hand, arm
- Choking
- Shooting
- Locking in a room
- Standing too close
- Stopping from leaving
- Restraining in any way
- Picking them up
- Holding or hugging when unwanted
- Pointing finger, poking
- Murder
- Hitting with objects
- Tickling
- Spitting

Sexual
- Forcing sex (rape)
- Total lack of intimacy
- Forcing certain positions
- Total lack of intimacy
- Sleeping around
- Hounding for sex
- Intimidation by knowledge or reputation
- Retaliating by refusing sex
- Put downs
- Being rough
- Using sex as basis for argument

- Treating someone as a sex object
- Pornography
- Forcing people to have sex with others

Financial
- Withholding money
- Spending money foolishly or beyond means
- Not spending money on special occasions, e.g. their birthday
- Making the decisions in terms of how money is spent

Environmental
- Locking them in
- Taking the phones with you to work
- Slamming doors
- Breaking things
- Throwing objects
- Turning the stereo/TV up loud
- Harming pets
- Throwing their clothes out
- Ripping their clothes

Social
- Not taking responsibility for children
- Embarrassment in front of children
- Putting down or ignoring in public
- Accusing them of sleeping
- Not saying what is on your mind
- Never really forgiving
- Lying

- Accusing them of sleeping around
- Treating them as a child
- Putting them on a pedestal
- False accusations
- Raising your voice with them
- Agreeing with them even though you don't
- Making them fearful
- Putting them or their family down
- Starting arguments
- Not letting them see their friends
- Using a continual joke or putdown about them with others
- Choosing friends or family over them
- Using kids as a weapon
- Abusing children physically or sexually
- Not taking them out
- Keeping them busy in the kitchen, e.g. during a party
- Change of personality with others
- Not being nice to their friends
- Making a "scene"

Emotional/Verbal/

Psychological
- Insulting
- Yelling
- Name calling
- Verbal threats
- Intimidation
- Playing "mind games"
- Overpowering their emotions
- Brainwashing

- Bringing up old issues and arguing with them
- Putting them down for things they have done in the past
- Inappropriate expression of jealousy
- Turning around a situation against them
- Laughing in their face
- Silence
- Walking away from them in a discussion
- Finding and verbalizing their faults
- Comparing them to others to conform to a role
- Overtly sarcastic or critical
- Lack of consideration for their opinion
- Trying to get last word in
- Pre-violence cues
- Isolation, e.g. not telling them what you are doing
- Refusing to do things with them
- Getting your own way
- Pressuring them
- Not coming home
- Real or suggested involvement with another person
- Manipulation
- Annoying mannerisms, e.g. snapping fingers
- Saying "Do you remember what
- happened last time"
- Making threats to them about you, e.g. killing yourself

24